TRANSFORMED BY THORNS

DR. GRANT MARTIN

Corky

Presented By
Scripture Press Ministries
Glen Ellyn, Illinois, USA

VICTOR BOOKS a division of SP Publications, Inc.
WHEATON. ILLINOIS 60187

Offices also in
Whitby, Ontario, Canada
Amersham-on-the-Hill, Bucks, England

AUTHOR'S NOTE: All names and other distinctive identifying information has been changed whenever reference has been made to former clients.

Recommended Dewey Decimal Classification: 248.4
Suggested Subject Heading: CHRISTIAN LIFE

Library of Congress Catalog Card Number: 84-52044
ISBN: 0-89693-397-0

CONTENTS

*To my wife, Jane, who
has loved me through all of our
shared thorns.*

PREFACE

Most of us have, at least secretly, wished for perfection. We may have yearned that somehow our human inadequacies would disappear. The fact is, we all have enduring weaknesses. While it would be nice to be problem-free, no one has yet succeeded. We face the choice of denying our human limitations, feeling sorry for ourselves, or learning profitable emotional lessons from our problems.

We can learn even if our weaknesses remain. God does not expect us to change every inadequacy into a strength. Rather, He allows us to learn from failure. We so often look ahead and pray for things to improve, failing to see the value of the immediate experience in light of God's total plan.

The major point of this book is that victorious Christian living is not achieved by the elimination of problems. Rather, our freedom comes by applying victorious principles to the problems. The goal is application, not elimination.

My premise is that we can grow and mature while we are right in the middle of problems—not when the pain is past. Even the recurring aggravations of stress, depression, anxiety, low self-esteem, and anger can be not only barriers, but vehicles to victory.

Yes, it would be nice if we could overcome or eliminate our shortcomings. Thorns are not comfortable and are seldom beautiful. Yet we can learn from them. Like sandpaper, weaknesses help to polish our potential as persons when God is permitted to do the polishing.

God indeed has provided creative patterns by which we can grow in our struggle with the problems of being human.

Grant L. Martin

ONE

*"I cannot carry
all these people by
myself; the burden is
too heavy for me"*
(Num. 11:14).

WHY TALK ABOUT THORNS?

"I have headaches almost every day! My back hurts so bad I could scream! I lost my temper at staff meeting again. I feel like crying all the time. What's the matter with me? I think I'm going crazy."

Kathy was confused and deeply discouraged, yet there seemed to be no reason for her despair and irritability.

"People tell me I am a natural leader. I guess I'm attractive enough. But I feel ugly inside and out. I used to enjoy working with young people. I really feel I could have a ministry through music. But lately I'm ready to quit. I guess I just don't have what it takes."

Kathy's good looks, musical ability, and outgoing personality gave observers the impression she was on top of it all. But deep down, where no one could see, Kathy's emotions were in total chaos.

In spite of her radiant smile and apparent enthusiasm, Kathy had grown increasingly aware of feelings, fears, and frustrations beyond her control. Prickly thorns had invaded the garden of her life. Weaknesses had begun to destroy her usefulness and beauty.

All of us face weaknesses and problems in our lives—perhaps less severe than Kathy's, perhaps more. One way or another, it's likely each of us experiences frustration in dealing with such things as depression, stress, or anger.

Yet it is possible to find growth, even in the midst of thorns. It may *sound* impossible, but it *can* happen. Problems can be used as stepping-stones to maturity.

Kathy felt the pain of her inadequacies. Symptoms demanding attention included: headaches and backaches, crying spells, temper outbursts, and feelings of depression. She could have attempted to ignore the problem or tried to make excuses.

Kathy wisely chose, however, to try to understand her weakness. Bittersweet feelings resulted. Looking at ourselves honestly is sometimes very unflattering. This was true in Kathy's case. Pitying herself, blaming God, and finding fault with others were tempting excuses. But Kathy eventually found that a more honest approach allowed God's power to function in her life.

What worked for Kathy can work for you! Low self-esteem, worry, and anxiety can be opportunities for you to grow also!

LEARNING FROM OUR THORNS

Three steps were involved in Kathy's experience. First, she had to acknowledge the presence of weakness in her life. This required a good look at herself—the anger about the lack of cooperation from her co-workers, the depression, lack of vitality, and hostile attitude. These negative attributes had to be faced. Ignored problems may become the greatest weakness of all.

Kathy's headaches and backaches came from being as mad as a hornet, but turning most of the sting on herself! Admitting her weakness and not blaming others for her problems became a giant step toward solving her dilemma.

Second, Kathy started exploring the source of her weakness. Her roots of anger led back to childhood and a hostile, competitive relationship with her father. Kathy's father controlled her primarily by fear. Scoldings, threats, and criticism were all she heard. He seldom complimented her, but continually challenged her to do better. Consequently, Kathy learned to be defensive and very competitive. Never permitted to enjoy an achievement, she seldom found satisfaction in goals already accomplished.

Kathy also faced disappointment in her dating experience. Young men were initially attracted to her, but were subsequently made to feel unwelcome. They interpreted Kathy's competitive nature as hostility and defiance. So they left her alone. They didn't want to get stung by an angry female.

After several months of counseling, her resistance to the expectations and requests of others became more understandable. Kathy began to see reasons for her feelings. They didn't happen just by chance, but were caused by her thoughts and beliefs. Though a gifted musician, she hated being *expected* to lead the singing at a church service or social event. She enjoyed simply being a participant sometimes; she didn't always want to be the leader. Yet Kathy saw she had allowed herself to be placed in a double bind. Every time someone would say, "Kathy, why don't you sing for us?" she would—smiling and sounding great. Inside, however, her stomach was tied in knots.

Kathy learned she could change her resentful thought patterns which had created the uproar inside her smiling profile. When her thinking changed, the negative impact of anger in her life was reduced.

The third step was being transformed by her thorns. Kathy realized God could help in spite of her weakness. Using her awareness and understanding, Kathy made a deliberate choice which eventually freed her from the headaches and moody spells. Her lessons included learning how to say no when the occasion demanded it. Some real, not plastic, roses began to flower among the thorns. Kathy learned to accept and love herself with no strings attached. Just because her father had attached conditions to his love was no reason for Kathy to treat herself the same way.

She also learned the important place of forgiveness in the healing of thoughts and feelings. Kathy finally communicated her feelings and intentions to her father. She asked his forgiveness for the accumulated bitterness. She also asked God's forgiveness and experienced His freedom.

This inner acceptance allowed a noticeable release from frustration and irritability. She saw more clearly how God was working in her life. She really did have a ministry to people! There was a master plan after all!

While working through these circumstances, Kathy continued to have very much the same personality. But she had more of a balance. Kathy persisted in making mistakes. But she learned errors can be forgiven.

God loved her for who she was, not just for how well she performed. He could use her, even with her imperfections. She learned to trust Him, even when she couldn't trust herself. Now she could

9

make and maintain friendships. But more importantly, she was learning to rely on God as her friend! She found she didn't have to panic or feel guilty when she made a mistake.

God teaches us in an atmosphere of love, not condemnation. Because of His love, a transformation took place in Kathy's thinking. By the renewal of her mind (Rom. 12:2), her thorns became learning opportunities which brought her personal growth!

SOCIETY SAYS WE CAN BE PERFECT

We all have a basic anxiety about our ability to handle life's challenges. We never escape it. As children we struggle with learning our multiplication tables. We worry about making friends. Will we make the cheerleading squad or the baseball team? We're anxious about what we're going to be when we grow up. After growing up, we worry about paying the bills. We bring children into this world and then we worry about *their* anxieties! The cycle never stops.

It's difficult just leading a normal life. But the pressure and propaganda of societal expectations often increases our anxiety. Radio, television, movies, and magazines try to convince us there is no excuse for being weak. In fact, it may even be disgraceful! Advertisements try to persuade us that success, good health, beauty, and happiness are available to everyone.

We are told we will make a hit, live with gusto, improve our love life, and have the shiniest floors in the neighborhood. The only requirements are that we use the driest deodorant, lather with the cleanest soap, drink the coolest beverage, and apply the clearest wax to our kitchen floor.

All of this propaganda tantalizes us with the assumption we should only be content with perfection. And it works! We spend millions of dollars trying to buy the American dream. The problem is that it *is* only a dream. The real truth is every one of us is imperfect. No matter what the beautiful people on TV say, we all have faults and limitations. Each of us has flaws, deficiencies, lack of opportunities, and weaknesses. Some seem small; some are major. Whoever we are, the bottom line is the same. Even if we do spend our hard-earned cash for these wonderful products, we will still be left with shortcomings or defects of personality, physiology, or social status. Even if we buy the new, improved, energy-efficient version, weakness will not be eliminated. Consequently, we are hurt and disillusioned when reality doesn't match the promises on the box.

The heartbreaking thing is that we assume everyone else is coming close to reaching the pinnacle of success. We make the mistake of believing the majority of our neighbors are actually reaching the heights of glory while we are not. But it's not true. The man who refinanced in order to install a hot tub, thus attempting to move to the top of the community status charts, is not necessarily happier than his spa-less neighbor. His only advantage is that he can soak his sorrows in 104-degree water that bubbles and foams around his ears. He's caught in the contradiction of trying to relax his body while worrying about how he is going to pay for his glorified teapot.

EVERYBODY HATES WEAKNESS

Not only does society glorify strength and perfection, but we go to great lengths to avoid weakness. Consciously or not, many people despise the retarded or slow learner, the clumsy athlete, or the forgetful senior citizen. Perhaps it's because we fear those who are different. Perhaps our rejection of them stems from a fear that their disabilities could befall us.

This fear and hatred of weakness starts early in life. Listen to the teasing taunts of grade-school children. The slow, chubby soccer player is ridiculed and jeered even though he may be the best reader in the class. Jokes are made about the slightest deviation—whether it's freckles, big ears, glasses, slow reading, lack of coordination, funny name, or accent.

From my own childhood, I recall Lowell who probably had a learning disability, but in the early '50s was called stupid and lazy. Lowell never did very well in school. He seemed more interested in trapping flies with an empty ink bottle than learning his multiplication tables. The kids teased Lowell a lot, but he was usually agreeable, friendly, and content in his own special world. And he was a pretty good first baseman!

Elva was probably retarded. She needed special classes and resources the school could not provide. So she was passed from grade to grade even though her skills remained at a lower level. Elva often was teased and treated very cruelly. Yes, she sometimes acted strange. But that was not sufficient reason for the unkind treatment she received.

These same dynamics appear in adult life. We dislike overweight people because of the struggle we may have with weight or self-control in some area of our lives. We denounce and join public outrage against pornography while failing to deal with our own uncontrolled sexual fantasies. We criticize an unemployed person collecting welfare, while at the same time avoiding a major motivation problem of our own. Our problem may be weak spiritual leadership in the home or unwillingness to take a Christian stand on a compromising situation at work. We become severely critical of weakness in the life of someone else, yet are blind to our own shortcomings. We continually fall into the trap of denying our humanness because we fear or hate it. But seldom do we make an honest appraisal that could provide a foundation for growth.

There are answers to this dilemma. We don't have to submit to the myth that only a select few will be able to become strong, competent, and successful. We do not have to feel the brass ring of life has been missed and our inevitable weaknesses and failures are overwhelming.

The future is far more hopeful. We have reason to be optimistic. We need to believe God when He promises abundant and meaningful lives (John 10:10) even though He has many lessons for us along the way. We must experience new ways of meeting the inevitable difficulties, frustrations, and personal inadequacies. Weakness is not an inevitable curse to deny, suppress, or project on others in order to maintain our sanity. Thorns can become beginning points, not just sore points.

WORM THEOLOGY AND POMPOUS POWER

Problems demand responses. Denial is one way to deal with them. Other possibilities are to try to overcome our problems, seek help, or give up.

Many people follow one of two approaches in attempting to handle their human limitations. These two forms of thinking are suggested by the following story.

A family had two young boys who were as different as night and day. Their dispositions were absolutely opposite. One boy was a confirmed optimist, the other a dreary pessimist. No matter what happened, the parents could count on one son seeing only the good in something and the other son only the bad.

The temperaments of the two lads were so different their parents consulted a psychologist for help in balancing out the boys' divergent qualities. The doctor drew on his extensive knowledge and recommended the following plan.

Christmas was coming, so the doctor suggested that the overly pessimistic son should be showered with presents. "Give him far more than he asked or dreamed," the psychologist said. "That will certainly overwhelm his negative outlook."

The eternal optimist, on the other hand, was to be given only one present. And it was to be very dull, boring, and inappropriate for a young boy. "When compared to his highly favored brother, your optimist will surely have some negative feelings for a change," the doctor added.

The plan was set into motion. On Christmas morning both boys came into the living room to see what Santa had brought. For the pessimistic son, there were dozens of presents. His stocking was loaded with candy and treats. Under the tree was every conceivable game and toy a young boy could want.

There was only one package for the optimistic boy. It contained only an old, frayed, leather horse halter the father had found in the attic.

"What did you get?" asked the cheerful brother as the pessimist looked over his mountain of gifts. With a glum countenance, the pessimist replied, "Oh, not much. Just the usual bunch of games, toys, clothes, and money. Nothing I really like. How about you?"

"Well," replied the optimist, "from the looks of this halter, I got me a pony, but he ran away! I'm so excited! Let's go find him!"

The respective outlook of those boys was unshakable!

Some of our attempts to deal with human weakness suffer from the same problem. The pendulum is pushed to one extreme of pessimism and defeat or the other extreme of naive optimism. Neither position contains the truth that can lead us to freedom.

There is truth and value in each of the positions to be described. But the goal is to have a balance that allows us to deal with the reality of sin and the hope of God's promises.

● *Weakness and worm theology.* This perspective of our human potential is represented in the hymn, "At the Cross," written by Isaac Watts:

Alas and did my Saviour bleed,
And did my Sovereign die,
Would He devote that sacred head
For such a worm as I?

Worm theology deals with human weakness by totally removing the value of self. "I am such a dreadful sinner that nothing good is in me. Everything I am has been corrupted by sin. In and of myself I'm no good at all. I'm as lowly as a worm."

Scripture and observation would seem to support the view that human nature should be despised. Jeremiah lamented, "The heart is deceitful above all things and beyond cure" (Jer. 17:9).

The Apostle Paul wrote, "I know that nothing good lives in me, that is, in my sinful nature" (Rom. 7:18).

Job, after catching a glimpse of the divine majesty, reacted by saying, "But now my eyes have seen You [God]. Therefore I despise myself and repent in dust and ashes" (Job 42:5-6).

Most of us can readily identify with Paul's statements recorded in Romans 7 because we have experienced temptation and have fallen prey to some of those enticements. Since this inclination to disobey God is so strong, it could be taken as evidence that we really are not much better than lowly fishing worms in His sight.

It's true that something in us needs to be put to death. That "something" is sin, the inclination to act contrary to the wishes of God. Every one of us has sinned (Rom. 3:23). And the sin in each of us needs to be hated and put to death (Rom. 6:23).

But here is a significant departure. God is not opposed to our essential nature. He made us. We are His sons and daughters. We are created in the very image of God (Gen. 1:27).

The worm theology approach to our weaknesses sees the tendency to sin as the "essential" part of our humanity. This position assumes that Paul's statement in Romans 7:18 ("nothing good lives within me") refers to the whole person. But Paul is only saying that the "sin" dwelling within him is worthless (Rom. 7:17). It is not man's total being that God despises.

One of the reasons God forbids murder is because His image dwells in all men. Christ came to free the image of God that resides in each of us (John 8:36). God wants His nature to be released for good.

If we make virtues of selflessness, self-reproach, and self-condemnation, we have no power to take up the cross as Christ commanded (Mark 8:34). While sin is undeniably present, God has provided a remedy. We are to acknowledge our shortcomings and ask forgiveness for sin. But we are not to make our human weaknesses the total focus, to the point we have no value. To dwell exclusively on the negative side of human nature is to ignore the whole purpose of God's grace and Christ's death. Feelings of despair and depression are certainly likely to develop if this negative view of self-worth is maintained.

A former client with a tragic childhood held this pessimistic view of life. Her parents were not able to communicate love in a way she could understand. She did many things as a young person for which she felt sorry. While her current circumstances seemed quite stable, she experienced strong feelings of depression and self-recrimination. She felt overwhelmed by her sinful past, as if destined to make evil choices. As far as she was concerned, God could not save her. Her strong feelings of anger toward herself and others convinced her she was beyond hope.

The worm theology approach would have been to agree with her belief. And the only help I could have provided under such a premise would have been to concur with her hopelessness and plead God's mercy.

Instead, we first clarified the facts of her condition. For her sin, forgiveness was the singular need. If she confessed, she could be absolutely assured that she was a child of the King (1 John 1:9). She could know her sins were forgiven as far as the east is from the west (Ps. 103:12). And, as a child of God, she was not subject to Satan's control (Ps. 125:2; John 16:33).

She struggled with these basic ideas. We discovered she was using her gloom and doom as a spiritual cop-out. Her overemphasis of her weakness had served to remove any personal accountability for growth. She was saying, in essence, "I'm so totally worthless that I am incapable of improving. I'm so bad, I can't be responsible for my actions or thoughts. I'll let my family worry about what to do with me."

God can protect and comfort His children. But we must take responsibility for our growth and discipleship. If we emphasize our personal inadequacies, we are contradicting God. His Word declares the gift of faith brings with it the grace to deal with life's challenges and thorns (1 Cor. 3:10; 15:10; 2 Cor. 12:9).

A balanced perspective on our humanness is essential. Worm theology does not give this necessary balance. Yes, we are definitely inadequate to meet life's problems with our own resources. Yet God wants to work through us. We are valuable creations, though our conduct is not perfect. We can be glad and thankful for many things. Given a balanced sense of value and worth, it is possible to take accountability for our spiritual growth.

● *Pompous power.* While worm theology emphasizes mankind's potential to sin, the power of positive thinking focuses on the potential to succeed. "I'd rather attempt to do something great and fail than attempt to do nothing and succeed," characterizes the positive self-talk of this line of thought.

While the pessimist reasons, "If I don't try, I can't fail," the positive thinker concludes, "If I don't try, I can't succeed."

The basic idea is that positive thoughts will bring about positive results. First, a person must establish good goals. Second, those goals must be affirmed strongly and frequently. Third, plans must be established which will help attain those goals. Fourth, the plans must be carried out conscientiously and diligently. We must "walk our talk."

Negative thinking must be avoided at all costs. If doubts creep in, positive phrases or images are to be used to eliminate the pessimism. Such affirmations include: "When you fail to plan, you plan to fail"; "You are God's project and God never fails"; "Change your thoughts and you can change your world."

Here is where the label "pompous power" can be applied. A puffed up sense of optimism is created when we assume that goals will *always* be achieved in a predictable manner. There is no guarantee life will always work out the way we hope. What happens when the inevitable time comes that our positive goals are not reached? Even if we believe and pray with all our hearts, all outcomes will not seem positive.

Don't get me wrong. It *is* valuable to establish a positive thought process. Scripture suggests that we will become what we think in our hearts (Prov. 23:7). We ought to fill our minds and hearts with as much power as possible. "For nothing is impossible with God" (Luke 1:37). "I can do everything through Him who gives me strength"

(Phil. 4:13). "For it is God who works in you to will and to act according to His good purpose" (Phil. 2:13).

This approach, however, can leave us with unreasonable expectations about how God works. Great frustration occurs when positive goals are set, but never materialize despite our best efforts. We will make mistakes. People do die. Children can run away. Banks have repossessed cars. Then unnecessary and false guilt sets in because we Christians are led to assume our lack of sufficient faith is the root of the problem.

We don't know God's total plan, so at a given point a prayed-for outcome may seem to be a failure. Depression, blame, anger, and rejection can result when we have tried too hard to use these positive thinking procedures and still meet defeat.

We must learn to deal with reality and not cover it over with nice—sounding ideas and promises. We need empathy, understanding, support, and love to deal with our crises, not unrealistic dreams or platitudes.

All too often I hear about someone whose child has died or who's lost his job or who's spouse has left. Unfortunately, the counsel to such a person has been, "In all things, give thanks." Forgotten is the fact that when a person has experienced a significant loss, he or she needs time to grieve, to experience the pain, and to eventually learn the lesson of the moment. Only then can he or she honestly give thanks to God and praise Him (1 Thes. 5:18).

Thorns hurt. We must not cover up the wound with a bandage before the injury has been identified and cleansed. To avoid inappropriate expectations about how God is going to work in our lives, we need to find the source and nature of our weaknesses. We may need to deal with the root causes of anger, lack of forgiveness, or questions about self-acceptance and purpose in life before we can profit from affirmations or positive-thinking strategies. To jump naively into energetic goal-setting without identifying what led up to the sense of loss, anger, and self-defeat is like giving a prescription without a diagnosis. If we quickly put a bandage over the wound without cleansing it first, infection will cause bigger problems later.

Some years ago a Christian family suffered a tragic automobile accident. The husband and two children were killed, leaving only the wife. The new widow was surrounded with attention and concern.

17

During the initial stage of numbness, everybody told her how well she was handling her grief. She hadn't cried much. No anger was expressed. But after a time, she was trapped. Her true feelings didn't dare be shown then because she had a new role to live up to. Her life was a model of Christian valor, strength, and apparent serenity.

Because this woman appeared to be coping so well, she was asked to speak to groups about how God had upheld her during her sorrow. Her words were always radiant and positive.

A year and a half later, she was hospitalized with severe ulcers. Her body was paying the price of stored anger and tension. She was living out a charade. She had not been allowed to experience her grief or to share her feelings with someone who understood and listened. She had kept up that ridiculous public pretense of confidence while her stomach took the brunt of the anger she couldn't outwardly express.

The wound was never cleansed, just covered over with unfeeling, superficial phrases of piety. Denying the reality of the hurt almost always leads to further complications.

CONTRASTS BETWEEN WORM THEOLOGY AND POMPOUS POWER

God *does* provide strength and comfort. We *can* find peace in tragedy. But it doesn't come by denial. We must face the situation honestly and squarely. Sometimes strong feelings will come to the surface. But cleansing occurs only when we are honest with ourselves. Placing unreasonably positive expectations on ourselves and on God only aggravates the pain.

There is truth in both the worm theology and positive thinking approaches to our weaknesses. There is danger, however, in the extreme application of either. The extreme negative perspective denies the presence of the image of God in each of us, which results in our avoiding accountability for growth and change.

Positive thinking, in the extreme, denies the presence of sin and weakness in human endeavor, which can prevent real ministry and healing from taking place.

Neither of these forms of denial is helpful. We must have a viewpoint that acknowledges sin and also appropriates the image and grace of God in our daily lives. David gave us a picture of this balance when he acknowledged his sin with Bathsheba: "Surely I have been a sinner from birth, sinful from the time my mother conceived me" (Ps. 51:5).

But David went on, after claiming God's unfailing love and great compassion (51:1), to look at the lessons that God had in store. "You teach me wisdom in the inmost place" (v. 6). "Create in me a pure heart, O God, and renew a steadfast spirit within me" (v. 10). "Then I will teach transgressors Your ways . . . and my mouth will declare Your praise" (vv. 13, 15).

There was no doubt about the sin of adultery David had committed. But once confessed and forgiven, he was freed to teach others and sing God's praises because of the renewed spirit within him. That same promise is available to each of us regardless of our circumstances!

TWO

"Have mercy upon me,
O Lord; for I am weak"
(Ps. 6:2, KJV).

THORNS ARE
HERE TO STAY

A young boy complained to his older sister about losing almost all of his baseball games during the past season. Attempting to cheer him up, the sister advised, "Remember, Timmy, you learn more from your defeats than your victories."

To which Timmy replied, "Well, I guess that makes me the smartest baseball player in the whole world."

Timmy was not happy with these wonderful lessons he was supposed to have learned from his losing season. His desire was to win. He wanted to be successful enough to have bragging rights on his block. But his desire was frustrated. Now Timmy would have to wait until next year to help improve his team's win-loss record. Meanwhile, he would wonder what he could possibly learn from having a batting average of .115.

A thorn is any human condition or tendency that interferes with our ability to accomplish goals. In the Bible, the metaphor of thorns expresses the idea of fruitlessness or frustration of effort (Gen. 3:18; Num. 33:55). Thorns were sometimes used as evidence of God's judgment of the ungodly (Nahum 1:10) or of sheer misfortune (Ezek. 2:6).

The destructive nature of thorns was expressed graphically in several parables that Jesus told (Matt. 13:7; Mark 4:7; Luke 8:7), along with the reference to their inability ever produce fruit (Matt. 7:16).[1]

THORNS ARE HUMAN WEAKNESSES

The terms *thorns* and *weakness* are used interchangeably in this book. Weakness is the inability to cope. It's an unsatisfactory handling of life's challenges and problems. Weakness is illustrated in the experience of the patient who went to her doctor complaining of anxiety, fearfulness, and uncertainty. She told the doctor about her eight children and a husband who was seldom home. She added that she frantically chaired three or four church committees, was president of the PTA, and a Red Cross volunteer. After describing additional symptoms of hot flashes, headaches, and forgetfulness, she asked the doctor, "What's wrong with me?"

The doctor, drawing on years of medical training and experience, said, "Ma'am, there are over forty miles of nerves in the human body. Now, in your case, that means you have 211,200 feet of the *frazzles*."

The doctor's diagnosis may not sound very scientific, but it comes close to describing the tension many of us have experienced. At times we all feel pulled in many directions. We know what it's like to feel tired and apathetic. But the clothes have to be washed anyway. Sometimes the struggles of life make us very weary. We worked late on the income taxes, but still have to commute one hour to work the next morning and face a classroom of seventh-graders who dare us to teach them anything about U.S. History.

Anytime we find ourselves doing less than an adequate job of coping with day-to-day frustrations, we are struggling with the thorns of weakness.

In the New Testament, the Greek word for weakness is *asthenia*. It is used in 2 Corinthians 11:30 where the Apostle Paul wrote: "If I must boast, I will boast of things that show my *weakness*" (italics mine).

Paul used the concept again when he wrote, "But He [the Lord] said to me, 'My grace is sufficient for you, for My power is made perfect in *weakness.*' Therefore I will boast all the more gladly about my *weaknesses*, so that Christ's power may rest on me" (2 Cor. 12:9, italics mine).

The scriptural word for *weakness* is very similar to our English medical terms, *anesthesia* and *anesthetic*, and conveys the idea of powerlessness or feebleness, the presence of a malady or frailty. It means to be impotent, sick, or without strength. It is also found in

Scripture as the word *infirmities*.

But almost more important than the meaning of weakness is our perception of it. We are the ones who determine whether or not our adjustments to problems are satisfactory. The major ingredient is not what other people think about us, but what we believe to be true. Remember Kathy from chapter 1? She was seen by others as happy and productive, yet her own judgment about her adjustment to life was far less positive.

We can't omit completely, however, the observations and impressions of others. Sometimes our family or friends see our weaknesses before we do. For example, if I were to continually criticize other people, I would certainly be showing a sign of weakness, even if I were blind to it. Eventually that weakness will catch up to me. My attitude will cause other people to be hurt and I may lose many of my friends. A time of reckoning will come. That's why personal awareness is such an important ingredient in learning lessons from our weaknesses. Sometimes it takes an abrupt and dramatic turn of events to see the light. The weakness has been there all along. And our contentment and joy have been reduced because of it.

THORNS HAVE ALWAYS BEEN HERE

Some sage has commented that in this day and age it takes nerves of steel just to be neurotic. While that may be true of the twentieth century, our problems didn't begin with the advent of the computer, television, video games, or Monday night football. The Bible is full of people who experienced thorns. Let's look at a few.

• *Moses.* Besides being a reluctant leader, Moses couldn't even impress his father-in-law, Jethro, who told him he wasn't doing a good job (Ex. 18:17-18). Moses expressed this lack of self-confidence later when he complained, "I cannot carry all these people by myself; the burden is too heavy for me" (Num. 11:14).

Moses must have also had the weakness of a quick and fiery temper. Remember when he killed the Egyptian (Ex. 2:11-12); when he threw down the tablets containing the Ten Commandments (Ex. 32:19); when he showed his impatience by striking the rock twice to get water (Num. 20:11). Though God used Moses in a mighty way, Moses' weakness of anger kept him from going into the Promised Land (Num. 20:12).

● *Abraham*. The spiritual pilgrim of the Old Testament was chosen by God to become the father of a new generation. Abraham was promised divine favor, great posterity, and that he would become a blessing to all the families of the earth. Because of his remarkable faith and obedience, Abraham is listed in the Hebrews 11 roll call of the heroes of faith.

But that faith did not develop overnight. Abraham was one of the Bible's greatest worriers. Abraham worried that foreign kings would covet his beautiful wife and kill him to get her (Gen. 12:12-13; 20:11). He worried about shortages of grazing land for his animals (Gen. 13:6-8), about retaliation (Gen. 15:1), about a lack of an heir (Gen. 15:2-3), about God's possible inability to honor His covenant (Gen. 16:1-4), and about God's intent to destroy Sodom and Gomorrah (Gen. 18:23-33).

In spite of God's promises, Abraham worried that he and Sarah were too old to bear children. After the birth of Isaac, Abraham worried that God wouldn't know which of his two sons to use in fulfilling the promise of many descendants (Gen. 21:11).

This is a side of Abraham we don't often talk about. Abraham was susceptible to the very human thorns of worry and anxiety. He grew from his experiences, but he was not always a hero of faith. God saw in Abraham the potential for greatness. And because of Abraham's obedience, he was eventually able to reach it.

● *David*. King David had many ups and downs. He acknowledged his weakness with these words: "And today, though I am the anointed king, I am weak, and these sons of Zeruiah are too strong for me" (2 Sam. 3:39).

David often had to confess sins to God. "I have sinned greatly in what I have done. Now, O Lord, I beg You, take away the guilt of Your servant. I have done a very foolish thing" (2 Sam. 24:10).

As great and popular as David was, he made foolish errors, yielded to temptation, and experienced severe depression and self-doubt. Human weakness was very much evident in his life.

● *Elijah*. Called the Prophet of Fire, Elijah was one of the more unique and dramatic characters in the Bible. We will talk more about him in our discussion of stress. Elijah probably experienced as much stress in his life as anyone has ever faced. He lived alone in the desert, appeared before a hostile king, opposed the major religious leaders of the land, antagonized the king's wicked wife, and then had to run for his life to escape her wrath.

After all of this, Elijah collapsed in a depressed heap out in the desert again, discouraged and despondent to the point that he asked God to let him die. " 'I have had enough, Lord,' he said. 'Take my life; I am no better than my ancestors' " (1 Kings 19:4).

Elijah was very familiar with the human conditions of overwhelming stress, depression, and poor self-esteem.

● *Christ's disciples.* Even the disciples had human infirmities. We see in Luke 9:46 and 22:24 that some of them were so filled with pride that they argued about who would be the greatest in the kingdom.

The problem of bigotry or jealousy showed itself in the disciples when they forbade someone to cast out demons, even though he was doing it in Christ's name. Because he wasn't a member of the "in" group, they apparently suspected his motives (Luke 9:49).

James and John showed vindictiveness when they were denied rooms in a Samaritan village. Both of them were ready to have Jesus order down fire from heaven to burn up the discriminatory innkeeper and his prejudiced neighbors. Of course, Jesus refused to do so, stating He came to save men, not destroy them (Luke 9:52-56, KJV).

We see very real human weakness in the disciples just prior to Christ's crucifixion. When Jesus could have used the support and encouragement of His disciples, they went to sleep on the job! (Matt. 26:40) It's hard to believe. The major purpose for which Christ came—to die for the sins of all mankind—and they were catching a few extra minutes of sleep.

I can't help but wonder if the psychological thorn of denial wasn't at work within Peter, James, and John. Jesus had foretold that Peter would deny Him three times before the rooster had crowed the next morning (Matt. 26:34). When Jesus spoke, Peter and the rest of the disciples forcefully denied they would ever offend their Lord (Matt. 26:35). But at the same time, they knew Jesus was always right. He could read the thoughts of people. He hadn't been wrong in his predictions yet. You can imagine the disciples' internal conflict—claiming two contradictory beliefs simultaneously.

25

Christ was "sorrowful and troubled" that Passover Eve (Matt. 26:37). He told the three disciples, "My soul is overwhelmed with sorrow to the point of death" (Matt. 26:38). Jesus then asked Peter, James, and John to stay with Him while He prayed in the Garden of Gethsemane.

You would think the severity of Christ's words and feelings would be intense enough to keep them involved. Their Lord, who had healed the sick and performed numerous miracles, was showing signs of depression and sorrow. But the disciples went to sleep anyway.

As close as these men were to the life and ministry of Jesus, they were emotionally unprepared for the events of the next few days. So they stuck their heads in the sand, denied the reality and pressure of their Lord's emotional and spiritual battle, and went to sleep. This is a clear example of weakness.

• *Paul.* The Apostle Paul had a "thorn in the flesh," which he mentioned in a letter to the church at Corinth (2 Cor. 12:7).

In the original language, the Greek word for *thorn* means a pointed piece of wood or a sharp stake, a bodily annoyance or disability. It probably referred to some type of constant bodily ailment or infirmity.[2]

Many have speculated on the nature of Paul's thorn. Some think it was epilepsy. Others suggest malarial fever. Still another suggestion is migraine headaches. Most frequently mentioned is that Paul had severe eye problems. It is possible an eye disease gave him occasional great pain and may have made him repulsive to look at. We really don't know for sure. Whatever it was, the thorn was significant enough that Paul had repeatedly asked God to deliver him from the problem.

God answered Paul as He frequently answers us. He did not take away the problem, but gave Paul the strength to bear it. Paul carried his thorn as a continual reminder of his human weakness and learned that the purposes and strengths of Christ were made clearer because of it (2 Cor. 12:8-10).

These examples underscore the fact that weakness is not escaped, even by biblical heroes. Even those who actually walked and talked with Christ experienced thorns. Still, God was able to use them mightily to spread the Good News of the Gospel. In fact, I wonder if the presence of human weakness isn't actually necessary for God to accomplish His purposes. If one is never inadequate, there would be no need to depend on God.

The same idea applies to our lives today. Victorious Christian living does not occur by the elimination of problems, but by learning how to apply biblical principles to them.

• *Charles Spurgeon.* Elizabeth Skoglund, in her book, *Coping*, describes the severe problems with depression experienced by the famous nineteenth-century preacher, Charles Haddon Spurgeon. Called the Prince of Preachers, Spurgeon became pastor of one of the largest churches in London at age nineteen. He published over 3,500 sermons and authored 135 books before his death in 1882 at the age of fifty-seven.[3]

Thousands of people came to hear Spurgeon preach. His ministry was deep and profound, yet countless times he struggled with severe heaviness of heart. His depression and poor physical health often kept him away from the pulpit.

> In the days of his greatest preaching in the Tabernacle, Spurgeon was often in despair and even thought of quitting, for he felt that his illness too often kept him from the pulpit. Fortunately the leaders of the church felt differently. They preferred Spurgeon with all of his frequent absences to any other man, even one who could be in the pulpit every time the church met. And so Spurgeon stayed. Yet his swollen hands and tired body made him an old man while he was yet young.[4]

The thorn of depression was a major component in the life of this great man of God. "Spurgeon was weak, yet strong. Ill, yet triumphant. He had emotional problems, but they only refined him into the finest of gold which bore the image of that Great Refiner of souls."[5]

Thorns have not disappeared with time. The fact that one of every four marriages ends in divorce is evidence many men and women today have trouble coping with the stress and strain of relationships and commitment. There's nothing wrong with the institution of marriage, but the weaknesses of selfishness and anger have destroyed many families.

I have talked with missionaries who have not been able to get along with coworkers and had to be reassigned. I recently talked to a divorced missionary couple where the husband had beaten his wife because he was unhappy with her preparations for hosting a Bible study. Somehow the contradiction of that situation never hit him until his wife left.

The range of human weakness and the stories of disaster are endless. There have been pastors who have committed adultery with members of their congregations. I have known men in spiritual leadership who have had affairs with their secretaries. Clients of mine have told me of temptations and actions from murder to child molestation. The only limit to sin and weakness is man's creativity in finding novel ways to break God's old commandments. There's nothing new under the sun when it comes to ways for thorns to cause frustration and grief.

The evidence is overpowering. There's no end to our thorns. No matter how sophisticated we get, our feelings of anger and depression remain. The calendar changes, but our infirmities do not.

IT HAPPENS EVERY DAY

Everyday experiences remind us that weakness is here to stay, that the tendency of human nature is to repeatedly make wrong choices. A common weakness faced by all of us at one time or another is pride.

Several years ago, a friend, John, and I went on a ten-day backpacking trip into the rugged Olympic Mountains of western Washington. The purpose of the course was to teach outdoor leadership skills ranging in complexity from meal preparation and map reading to mountain climbing and foul weather survival.

Though the trip was in May, most of the activities took place at 5,000 to 7,000 feet elevation, and thus snow fell at least part of each day. After the first day, we walked and camped totally on three to five feet of snow. The overnight temperatures dropped to as low as seventeen degrees, soundly testing my newly purchased down sleeping bag.

John and I were the oldest members of our expedition. The rest were mostly church youth leaders under thirty. One of the goals of the course was to provide leadership opportunities in an unfamiliar environment. On the last day out, John and I were assigned the task of leading the group from our last high-altitude campsite back down to our beginning point.

We devised several experiences to help each group member evaluate the course. Since we were both "highly trained" individuals with doctoral degrees, we were probably a little anxious to show the rest of these "kids" just how wise and capable we were. Our egos needed strengthening since we often had been struggling to keep up with the fast hiking pace of the group's younger members.

Of course, with all of this education and knowledge, John and I felt confident in our abilities to read the map, determine the compass headings, and navigate the best course to get us back to dry clothes and hot showers. *No problem!* we thought. Well, it didn't work out that way. You see, most maps don't include instructions for finding a trail when it is under five feet of snow! Maps are made in the summertime when the terrain is out there for all to see, not hidden by millions of tons of crunchy, wet, white stuff.

Our problems began just after John and I confidently marched to the front of the line (for the first time in days!) and fearlessly commanded the group, "This way!" Everything seemed fine. We crossed a meadow at the foot of a tall peak, just as indicated on the map. Then things began to get difficult. The meadow ended and the tree line on the far edge appeared. The question was, "Where does the trail enter the trees?" John and I suddenly realized we had lost the trail. It was somewhere five feet under us, but obliterated by the snow. There was no gap in the trees, no marker, no signpost, nothing we could use as a reference point. We knew the general direction in which we wanted to go. But keeping to the trail would make the trek much easier. If we could find it, that is!

We told the rest of the group to take a break. After all, we had been walking for thirty minutes! While the group was taking this hardly needed rest stop, John and I checked our maps and made our navigational calculations. We felt certain we would have everything under control after a few minutes of high-powered thought.

Wrong again! Our secure attitude began to waver a bit when we couldn't find our precise location on the map. Neither could we pinpoint the two-foot-wide trail that would take us back to warm beds and the first solid, hot food in eight days. Thus we resorted to our basic instinct—"trial and error."

In our most logical manner, we tried to organize the rest of the group into search parties to fan out up and down the side of the clearing to locate the trail. At that point, we lost total control of the group. Everyone went in different directions. Nobody knew where anybody else was going. Different people went over the same area and some areas were skipped. The confusion and loss of leadership lasted for several hours as we tried to find that elusive trail.

After numerous wild goose chases and false alarms, we finally got most of the group together and decided to head off in the general direction of camp. But by then, we had lost most of our confidence and all of our authority.

Later the trail was rediscovered again. We safely descended the mountain and arrived at base camp fairly close to the intended time. John and I suffered a few bruises to our egos and the rest of the group didn't miss the opportunity to give us some good-natured needling. No real harm had occurred.

In one insincere, last-ditch effort, we tried to persuade the rest of the group the whole experience was really a planned exercise in group dynamics. John and I said we knew all along exactly where the trail was located, but we were merely pretending confusion to see how the group would handle the frustration and indecision. For some reason, they were not convinced!

Though a bit embarrassed, John and I suffered no lasting loss. In fact, we learned something about handling a group in a disorganized, mildly hostile environment. We also were reminded that God isn't limited by compass markings or forest service guidelines when He sends down snowflakes.

But more than that, we learned anew the meaning of the words— "Pride goes before destruction, and a haughty spirit before stumbling" (Prov. 16:18, NASB). The thorns of overconfidence and pride were made uncomfortably clear.

In summary, we can say a thorn occurs any time we find ourselves unable to cope in a satisfying way. Weaknesses can appear in the physical, emotional, social, intellectual, or spiritual aspect of our experiences.

If we are honest, the existence of weaknesses are common to us all. Try as we might, it's hard to deny our struggles with such things as pride, envy, anger, poor self-esteem, and stress.

The bad news is that thorns will always be with us. The good news is that God has something to teach each one of us in the middle of those thorns. As we will see, growth doesn't occur by eradication of problems, but by learning to apply godly principles to them.

THREE

*"We will in all things
grow up into Him
who is the Head"*
(Eph. 4:15).

GROWTH: KEEPING AHEAD OF THE WEEDS

The newspaper headline announces another horror story: "Child Kept Captive." The grim details unfold.

Child Protection Society workers today were called to the home of Mr. and Mrs. John Doe and discovered one of the worst cases of child abuse they had ever seen. Amid the most despicable circumstances, an animal-like young child was found locked in the attic of a home in a remote part of the county.

CPS workers report the room was absolutely filthy. There was only a mattress on the floor and piles of garbage and human waste accompanied the stench.

According to Mr. and Mrs. Doe, ages fifty-six and fifty-four, the seven-year-old child whom they call "Boy" has been restricted to the attic room without outside contact for six years. The Does, who claim to be the child's aunt and uncle, say they have had custody of the child since his parents were killed in an auto accident.

When asked about the cruel conditions, the Does defended their action by claiming the child was possessed of the devil and they were protecting other children from coming under his influence.

The child was taken to Children's Hospital, where medical personnel reported he was not able to speak and uttered only shrill screams.

Police are investigating possible criminal charges.

Though my example is fictitious, such events do occur. Think of the deprivation the child had experienced. No playmates. No cuddling or loving. Just a cup of water and junk food for years.

For no sane reason, the child was kept hidden from the outside world. As a tragic consequence, he never learned how to talk, play, run, or communicate except in grunts and animal sounds. The child was not toilet trained because he was never taught.

Such conditions had produced a severely handicapped child. Lack of environmental stimulation or tender loving care had created a human being who was stunted, perhaps beyond help, because normal growth was not allowed.

Any limitations to growth, voluntary or not, can result in tragic consequences. I have seen results firsthand. A client told me she had contracted some type of illness when she was about twelve years old. She didn't know what kind of illness had befallen her, but she did remember being restricted to the house for a year and a half! For eighteen months she wasn't allowed to see or talk to anyone but her parents. Strangely, she doesn't even remember being sick. As far as she was concerned, there was no reason for the extended quarantine.

Forced social isolation at such a critical developmental age kept her from learning how to properly get along with people. Her problems now with drug abuse, alcoholism, depression, and several suicide attempts were probably a result of that period of time when she was not allowed social contact. The normal ups and downs of adolescence, while frustrating, are necessary to build a strong person. My client missed out on a significant part of her maturation process and has paid a heavy price because of it.

If we are to learn valuable lessons from life's thorns, it is important to see the necessity of growing in social and personal adjustment.

What is growth? It's development or progress toward maturity. It is movement from one level to a higher measure of ability. A young child first learns to crawl, next to walk, then to run, and eventually to ride a bicycle. Growth occurs in emotional and spiritual ways as well as physical ones. We understand that physical growth must take place from the playpen to the baseball diamond. Emotional and spiritual growth follows the same patterns of practice and improvement. Or, at least, growth *should* take place within a normal, balanced person. That's what God intended.

Growth means movement forward. Lack of growth suggests a delay, impairment, or breakdown in the maturation process. A baby, for example, comes into the world totally dependent on others for survival. But in the course of growing up, that infant must learn how to meet most of its own needs. He or she must learn how to give as well as receive. A highly dependent or selfish person will have difficulty with the demands of adult life if he or she never progresses past childhood. It's true. We're young only once, but we can be immature indefinitely!

Another example of the necessity of growth can be seen in the condition of muscles after a period of disuse. When I was in the sixth grade, I broke a bone in my foot while playing baseball. My foot was in a cast for six weeks, but in my anxiety to get back on the ball field, it seemed like twelve. Once the cast was off, I had assumed I could put on my baseball shoes and pick up where I left off. Wow, was I surprised! When I climbed down off the table after the doctor had removed the cast, I tried to walk to the door and fell flat on my face! Those foot muscles were weak and atrophied after six weeks of disuse. I learned then and there, "If you don't use it, you lose it!"

THE GROWTH PRINCIPLE

Growth is absolutely necessary for physical and emotional well-being. And growth must take place in all aspects of our lives. Clients will frequently tell me:

"I'm bored with life."

"My job doesn't have any challenge to it anymore."

"Nothing has any meaning in my life."

A frequent issue these days is the housewife who no longer finds fulfillment in carting the children to baseball games and clipping discount coupons. The common complaints are:

"I'm not growing anymore."

"I don't feel my abilities are being used or recognized.'

"I feel trapped and worthless because I'm not doing anything of real value."

These comments highlight the basic principle about growth. Every individual, in order to function in an effective manner, must feel he or she is growing, producing, and creating in ways that are reinforcing, rewarding, and appropriate. All of us need to see growth or the potential for growth in our lives. If growth is not experienced, we feel frustrated or blocked. When this happens, inappropriate and undesirable forms of behavior can result. In extreme forms, some responses to a lack of growth are called mental illnesses.

If a person sees himself producing in ways that he feels are appropriate, his self-esteem will be positive. If the reverse is true, his self-image will be negative. With a low self-esteem, more barriers to growth occur and a downward progression is likely.

These are some of the reasons why growth is important. But it doesn't stop here. For the Christian, we have a responsibility to grow. In fact, the idea of growth was first described in the Word of God, not in psychology texts.

The basic cornerstone of Christian belief is the knowledge that the believer begins as a babe and continues growing and maturing in Christlike ways throughout his life. At least, that is what we are supposed to do!

Much of the Book of Hebrews is an exhortation to the new church to grow. The key word in Hebrews is *better*. The author strongly suggests the believer must leave the initial nourishment of milk as "a child" and grow into the "solid food" of the mature Christian (Heb. 5:12-14).

The author of Hebrews goes on to suggest we should "leave behind the elementary teaching about Christ and go forward to adult understanding" (Heb. 6:1, PH). Earlier, he had said it was time to become teachers of God's Word, not dull pupils (Heb. 5:12). We can't become teachers until first we pay attention to the lessons our Master intends for us to learn.

In Ephesians 4, Paul wrote about the spiritual gifts God gives us and the ways in which they are used to build up the body of Christ. After mentioning the various gifts, Paul went on to say, "Speaking the truth in love, we will in all things grow up into Him who is the Head, that is, Christ. From Him the whole body, joined and held together by every supporting ligament, grows and builds itself up in love, as each part does its work."

Notice the emphasis on growth. It has to happen for everything else to work properly. Growth is evidence of life within the body, be it our physical bodies or the fellowship of Christians.

Additional passages in Philippians 1:6, 2 Thessalonians 1:3, 1 Peter 2:2, and 2 Peter 3:18 also reflect the importance God places on the growth of each Christian. We were not created to be stagnant "bumps on a log." We were created to be dynamic, growing beings who desire to expand our understanding.

GOD WANTS US TO GROW

We hear about the need to become self-actualized, truly alive and self-fulfilled. It's not a new idea. Jesus fully understood the needs of man when He said, "I came that they might have life, and might have it abundantly," (John 10:10b, NASB).

God wants each of us to experience abundance and creativity. God created man as a perfect creature. But Adam and Eve sinned and that sin was passed on to us all. Our sinful nature predisposes us to violate God's will and separates us from that abundant life He promises. But God also provided a way to overcome sin through the person of His Son, Jesus Christ. Therein is the opportunity for each of us to accept Christ and make Him a meaningful part of our lives. Only through our faith and obedience are we able to enjoy self-fulfillment. This is not achieved because of our own merit, intelligence, or status, but because of God's grace, His help, and His guidance.

God wants us to grow. Every situation we experience is a growth opportunity. In our limited perspective, we don't always see potential for growth, but it is there. We have God's promise it will happen.

Think of the growth experiences throughout Israel's history. For forty years, the people wandered around the desert looking forward to the Promised Land. Now, that desert was no Palm Springs! It was dry and barren. No air conditioners or motor homes to keep them cool. But with all of its problems, the desert wasn't as bad as it might have been. God had taken marvelous care of His children. They had seen Him in miracle after miracle. They had been delivered from their oppression in Egypt. God had provided food and water. He had given clear signs to guide their travel.

Then the Children of Israel entered the Promised Land, which was flowing with milk and honey. Now surely their problems would be over. At least, that's what they anticipated. But things began to change in a way they didn't expect.

The pillar of fire by night and cloud by day no longer gave them direction. No more morning manna or quail outside their tents. Their shoes started wearing out for the first time; they were confronted by terrifying giants. Their leadership began to have second thoughts.

Gideon expressed a degree of panic about the turn of events. After being reassured by an angel that the Lord was with him, Gideon responded, "You've got to be kidding!" Actually, Gideon said, "But sir . . . if the Lord is with us, why has all this happened to us?" (Jud. 6:12-13) Gideon couldn't understand why, just when the journey was supposed to be over, events took a turn for the worse.

In spite of obstacles, the Children of Israel were exactly where God wanted them. God did not leave them. The miracles would not stop no matter how tall the giants.

In just the same way, we may not see how God's will is going to unfold. We look at our thorns and begin to lose hope. We tend to lose sight of God's ability to continue the maturation process despite the immediate circumstances.

Dr. C. Markham Berry discussed the transition period in the lives of the Children of Israel in the following way:

> The change experienced at the Jordan transition is not away from the power, love, and order of God, but away from the narcissism of childhood which insists these be demonstrated to *me*, in *me*, and for *me*. Spiritual adulthood is concerned with the miraculous power expressed more richly and deeply in showing the eternal character of His purpose in history. In other words, there is a shift from expecting God to make *me* healthy, wise, prosperous, holy, and free from suffering, to tuning in on the riches, wholeness, and might of *God*, which is what the show is really about. This will inevitably involve, for us as it did with Christ Himself, loneliness, suffering, weakness, illness, and even blindness. In the process, though, we will discover that His strength can be perfected in our weakness (2 Cor. 12:9) and that those things which once gave us reason for confidence in the flesh . . . now are

37

"counted as loss" to "gain Christ," which involves "the fellowship of His sufferings. . . . " (Phil. 3:4-16).[1]

A change from the self-centered "me" to more of an "other" perspective occurred for me while playing my clarinet during high school and college. I started playing the clarinet in the third grade. While never a great musician, I did become fairly competent from a technical point of view. As a result, I could play fairly difficult versions of hymns and songs. After I had played a solo which was filled with lots of complicated trills, fast runs up and down the scale, and so forth, I would get a few smiles and one or two compliments following the service. People would say, "My, that song must have been very difficult," or "Grant, you played so well tonight."

As I look back on it now, those folks may have felt obligated to say something. Their words certainly fed my hungry ego.

On the other hand, there were times when I would play a rather simple, but familiar old church hymn. People could recall the words as I played, and afterward many of them remarked how much they were touched by the musical message. At first, I couldn't understand. "How could they like that?" It wasn't very difficult. Anybody could have done it."

Then I began to see the difference. God was finally able to use me as an instrument to touch the hearts of people. Playing a difficult piece of music was just my way of showing off and was not really honoring to God. The honor was intended for me, not Him. But when I changed my motive and determined the theme of the worship service, selected music that complimented the message, and played with more attention to feeling and content, the results were far better. God was more likely to use the performance for others' benefit, not mine.

It took me a long time to recognize those lessons, but I now see it as growth. Like the Children of Israel crossing into Canaan, I experienced an adolescent stage of transition. I regret the pride initially present, but I'm grateful for the maturation that took place.

STAGES OF SPIRITUAL GROWTH

Seven stages of spiritual development can be described, which parallel the aging of man from child to adult. Recognition of these different steps in our spiritual maturation may help us evaluate our current status. From that point, we can set our sights for future growth.

Remember, spiritual development does not necessarily follow physical growth. One could be a young adult spiritually, yet fifty years old chronologically. Paul spoke of new believers as babes in Christ (1 Cor. 3:1). Thus, I am about to describe the entire progression of development, from naive unawareness about spiritual things to maturity in the implementation of the faith.

• *Early childhood*. The first stage of growth begins with the development of a conscience—the ability to know right from wrong. Conscience is universal. The definition of what is acceptable may vary from one culture to another, but rules regarding conduct are present everywhere.

An infant soon learns not to touch the candy dish on the coffee table. (Or else Mom learns to put all the pretty things away for a couple of years!) A toddler learns some behavior is permissible and some is punishable. Parents are the primary source of these do's and don'ts. Out of this environment, the child begins to develop a sense of morality. Because his thinking is very concrete, the major sources of moral development are the threat of punishment and the promise of rewards. The young child does not have any awareness of abstract concepts like honesty or neatness. He just knows that when he smeared Mom's lipstick all over the wall, he got spanked. So he decides it would be less painful not to do that again. On the other hand, it is nice to hear Dad's praises for a task well done.

Though very basic, this sense of morality leads to a limited and general awareness of deity. There is some higher being. Something exists bigger than himself. Aided by the comments and teachings of older persons, the child begins to know that there is someone called "God" out there.

As the frustrated four-year-old was heard to respond to his mother's request to wash his hands, "Germs and God! That's all I hear about in this house! And I've never seen either of them!"

• *Late childhood*. Gradually, the preteen child increases his spiritual awareness. Closely following the type of morality to which he has been exposed, the child begins to select values and attitudes which are consistent with his idea of God.

This is a time of searching and exploring, and the sources of influence at this stage are many. Peers, TV, movies, and teachers are added to the values modeled and taught by parents. Many people never grow past this stage in their spiritual development. The attraction of good times, personal freedom, and paths of least resistance hinders any additional inquiry about who God is and what He desires from man.

Through the influence of the Holy Spirit, the teaching of home and the church, and the example and testimony of others, some young people do move forward in their search. The person and message of Jesus Christ is examined and evaluated. If that message, the Good News of the Gospel, is received and accepted, the person moves to the next stage.

• *Adolescence.* Keep in mind a person can be thirty-five years old according to the calendar, but still enter the adolescent stage of spiritual development. This stage is one of commitment. It begins when a person makes a personal decision about his spiritual life, when Jesus Christ is received as the only way of salvation (John 14:6; Acts 4:12) through an individual act of faith. Understanding, acceptance, belief, and confession accompany this decision. The new life has begun! (Phil. 1:6)

• *Young adult.* When we realize there is more to Christianity than just the basics and become willing to grow, young adulthood is reached. Accompanying this phase will be an awareness of the needs around us—spiritual as well as social.

Unfortunately, many Christians have never reached this level of maturity despite Scripture's encouragement to put away childish things (1 Cor. 13:11), to not be content with a childlike understanding (1 Cor. 14:20), to know God's Word (1 Peter 2:2), and to strive after Christ's ideal (Eph. 4:13).

Solomon was said to have not only wisdom and understanding, but "largeness of heart" (1 Kings 4:29). This suggests a strong desire for the welfare of others, which is a measure of maturity.

This stage is a time of discontent. There is dissatisfaction with the status quo and a desire to reach out and touch others with the Good News of the Gospel. This desire to grow will also be accompanied by increasing spiritual discernment—the ability to know what is helpful for continued growth and what is not (Heb. 5:14).

The desire to grow and to reach out to others naturally leads to questions about God's plan and how each of us fits into it.

• *Adult.* The adult Christian is motivated to understand God's direction for his activities. The desire to grow, which began in the young adult phase, is now translated into efforts to establish conditions for fruit-bearing (John 15:16). Specific goals of demonstrating love, joy, peace, patience, kindness, goodness, faithfulness, gentleness, and self-control are established (Gal. 5:22-23).

The awareness of God's purpose for our lives—to bear fruit—then influences us to determine how to bring about that fruit in a practical way. How can the race of life be completed in a manner pleasing to God? (1 Cor. 9:24; Heb. 12:1)

The Apostle Paul wrote that a sign of maturity is the desire to "press on toward the goal to win the prize for which God has called [us] heavenward in Christ Jesus" (Phil. 3:14). Maturity here means being fully fit for running. It also means being informed and knowledgeable about the rules of the race (2 Tim. 2:5).

Being spiritually fit, conditioned in God's Word, receptive to possible pruning (John 15:2), and dependent on the leading of the Holy Spirit (John 16:13) are prime qualities of the Christian who has matured into the adult stage.

• *Mature adult.* The specific understanding and practice of how we are to participate in the mission of God's kingdom gives the mature adult Christian a sense of ministry. How our particular blend of interests, talents, gifts, and opportunities fit into the community of believers provides the refined perspective necessary for a mature understanding of that ministry.

We are called to be ministers of God (2 Cor. 3:6; 4:1), and we are all part of the priesthood of believers (1 Peter 2:5). The mature adult takes that responsibility seriously and combines it with a clear idea of how he fits into God's plan in his career, home, church, and community.

• *Elder.* The final stage of spiritual development applies to the wise, experienced Christian who has demonstrated sound judgment. The elder is perhaps older, because it takes time to acquire wisdom (Job 32:7). Wisdom, however, will always come from God, but not always from older men (Job 32:8-9).

It is this same biblically based wisdom (2 Tim. 3:15) that is the mature expression and example of fruit-bearing (James 3:17). Yet it is

41

available to all who ask (James 1:5).

The elder Christian has a clear perception of God's plan. He has skill and discretion in imparting spiritual truth (Col. 1:28), and his wisdom and understanding are demonstrated in his godly and upright living (James 3:13).

In many ways the elder is the transmitter of the faith, one who is looked to for example and instruction. His faith has been tried and tested, yet has emerged victorious (Rev. 2:10).

These seven stages are not fixed or rigid. But they do seem descriptive of the maturation process evident in the growing Christian. As you read about these stages, ask yourself, "Where am I? Could I be further along? What do I need to do to get going?"

GROWTH IS RISKY

Growing isn't easy. In fact, it can be downright scary because it requires us to take risks. The Children of Israel had promises about the land on the other side of the river, but they couldn't turn those dreams and promises into reality until they actually went into the land. They had to face the giants before the land could be theirs. Their biggest enemy was not the giants as much as it was fear itself.

Or take an example from the animal kingdom—the lobster. At certain times in development it's impossible for a lobster to grow larger because its hard shell is too tight. The only way a lobster can increase its size is to shed its outer covering at regular intervals. When the lobster begins to get too big for its britches, it looks for a reasonably safe place to rest while the shell comes off. The pink membrane inside becomes harder and harder and a new protective covering is formed. During this time (about six to eight weeks), the lobster is quite vulnerable. It can be eaten by a fish, tossed against rocks, or crushed very easily because of its lack of outer armor. In short, a lobster has to risk its life in order to grow.

Sometimes the risks in our lives seem awfully great. But the alternative is to smother in our old shell. We may be tempted to stay well within our comfort zone, where everything is familiar. But familiarity can suffocate vitality right out of existence.

Growth is essential. If we don't grow, we wither away. God in His wisdom wants us to grow and mature. It's good for us. God hasn't promised us a perfectly smooth ride down the river of life. But He has promised direction, strength, and support for any turbulent water along the way.

God alone can respond to the deep-rooted anguish we feel over our human limitations. Through Him we can accept our thorns, sometimes overcome them, and always learn from them. That's how we can keep ahead of the weeds!

FOUR

*"Apart from Me, you
can do nothing"*
(John 15:5).

GROWING
THROUGH STRESS

The screech of rubber tires on the pavement followed shortly there-
after by a crash and a thud jarred my concentration! This was not a
normal sound for our usually quiet neighborhood. My heart skipped a
beat. I had a heavy feeling in the bottom of my stomach as I threw
down the evening paper and ran to the front door of our home. All
was silent for a few seconds and then the loud screams of Lance, our
seven-year-old son, intensified my anxiety. My wife and I ran out the
door as Lance came running across the lawn.

"I got hit by a car! I got hit by a car!" he shouted between panic-
stricken sobs. Within moments, my observations and the comments
of quickly arriving neighbors verified Lance's words.

While riding his bicycle on the street in front of our house, Lance
had been hit and knocked off his bike onto the edge of our neighbor's
lawn.

Our first concern was for Lance's physical condition. While very
frightened, he had been able to get up and run back to the house. His
ability to move indicated there was apparently no serious injury. However, his ankle began to hurt as some of the initial shock wore off, so
later we took him to the hospital emergency room for examination.

My second thought was, "How did it happen? Where is the car that
hit him?" The bystanders, including our family baby-sitter, reported
seeing a neighborhood teenager speed down the street, hit Lance, and
drive away.

My reaction was anger. Hit and run! We had been complaining about this boy's reckless driving for months. Now my son was his victim!

The neighbors called the police. A few minutes later, however, the car returned to the scene and the boy acknowledged his participation in the accident. I was relieved that he came back, though still upset by his reckless behavior. I told him I would get back to him later and proceeded to take Lance to the hospital. X rays showed a chipped ankle bone, but nothing more serious. Thank the Lord! Just one very frightened seven-year-old who refused to ride a bike for six months.

Things began to settle down a few hours later when we returned from the hospital. A somewhat overcooked dinner was finally eaten and a semblance of routine and order began to reappear in the Martin household. The stress of the evening was beginning to dissipate.

STRESS DEFINED

Stress is a common term. We apply it to describe feelings caused by events such as a death in the family, financial crises, employment problems, a flunked test, a first date, or a flat tire on the freeway.

Stress occurs in many forms. It can be physical, like Lance's accident. Or it can be emotional, like giving a speech for the first time. Stress can be the result of a short-term crisis, or it can drag out for months.

Actually, stress is another word for adaptation or adjustment. Stress is our body's physical, mental, and chemical reaction to circumstances that frighten, excite, confuse, endanger, or irritate us.

There are two types of stress patterns—specific and general. A specific type of stress is the near miss on the freeway or the ferocious dog tearing at your ankle bone. Lance's bump by the speeding car was a specific stressor. It was traumatic for a short time, but after a few hours his heightened level of adjustment returned to normal. In other words, Lance's blood pressure, breathing rate, and adrenaline level went sky-high during the accident, but calmed down by bedtime. This kind of stress, while traumatic, is clear and specific. You know when it is over.

General stress is accumulative. The adjustment process is more likely to involve emotions linked to problems in day-to-day living. A typical day may go as follows: As usual, you pick the slowest line at the bank. You finally get waited on, try to cash a check, and find you are overdrawn by $200. Everybody within thirty feet hears the teller comment, "I'm sorry, Mrs. Roberts, I can't possibly cash your check because you're overdrawn again."

Embarrassed and angry, you return home to find a poor work notice in the mail from your son's teacher. Finally, your husband gets home and reports he may get laid off from his job any time now. This hasn't been a good day!

At each point of frustration, your body will react, in a moderate way, as it might if you were in obvious physical danger. In each situation, something important to you was threatened. Your life wasn't endangered, but your emotions or values were. Your body can't clearly distinguish between emotional and physical threats, so it adapts to each of the stressors as if to fend off physical harm. Since there is no immediate resolution to these more general threats, however, your body ends up in a constant state of battle.

If this state of tension continues, the whole body system will eventually become exhausted. Your level of functioning will deteriorate and with it your ability to cope. A burnout is in the making!

FRIEND OR FOE
Stress is impossible to avoid. But that's OK. Stress can be good for us; it can build muscle; it can prepare us to handle unfamiliar events. Stress will be a good teacher, however, only if we respond in a healthy manner. In our panic, we often resort to ineffective methods of conduct.

The potential for positive adjustment is present in every stressful situation. The primary goal in emergency room treatment, for example, is to remove interferences to survival so that the God-given adaptation process can take over. God has provided healing mechanisms in the body; the doctor merely tries to put the pieces back together so natural healing can take place.

God gave us the potential to cope with all kinds of stress if we can just remove the interferences to that positive adaptation. We must learn to apply the promise, "I can do everything through Him who gives me strength" (Phil. 4:13).

The Department of Asian Languages at the University of Washington confirmed the Chinese word for *crisis* is written by combining the characters for the words *danger* and *opportunity*. These characters are reproduced below.[1]

CRISIS = DANGER + OPPORTUNITY

Stress contains these same elements. If we learn to make the appropriate adjustment, stress is a friend or an opportunity that strengthens us for the next encounter. Handled poorly, stress can be an enemy that leads to emotional and physical destruction. The choice is ours. Stress can be an opportunity for growth, not just a thorn in the side.

DEALING WITH STRESS

● *Step 1—Awareness of what's happening to you.* You need to know stressors are present in your life before you can make the appropriate adjustments. There's no problem with awareness if a cement truck is about to run you down. Problems occur when stress accumulates little by little. We may find ourselves burned out without realizing we're in trouble. We become numb and insensitive to stressful events. After the seventeenth hassle of the day, who's counting?

Our body is usually the best source of information about a stress connection. A few years ago, I started waking up in the morning with very sore jaws. It wasn't clear to me what was wrong. I was about to call my dentist when something made me stop and take inventory. I asked myself the question, "My teeth are healthy, so what could be causing my jaws to hurt?"

Self-examination told me I was overloading the activity circuits. I had too many commitments in my life. Because of extreme tension, I was going to bed and clenching my jaws all night long.

That self-imposed pressure had continued until my body began to get fed up with the extra tension. My jaws were telling me, "Enough is enough."

Knowing why my jaws were hurting gave me some immediate relief. Over the next few weeks, commitments were completed or reduced and my overall stress level went down. My jaws stopped hurting. The message that my body was sending to my brain finally got through.

Listen to your body. It will tell you a lot about your stress level. The less in touch you are with your body, the louder it will have to yell to get your attention.

Use the following checklist to determine which of the signs might be used by your body when too much stress accumulates.

EMOTIONAL SIGNS

____ I become worked up and excited.

____ I worry too much.

____ I can't sleep.

____ I feel at loose ends.

____ I get forgetful and confused.

____ I sleep too much.

____ I become dizzy and disoriented.

____ I become grouchy and irritable.

____ I feel nervous.

INTERNAL SIGNS

____ My stomach gets upset.

____ My heart beats fast or irregularly.

____ I perspire a great deal.

____ My hands get clammy.

____ I become light-headed or faint.

____ I get hot and/or cold spells.

____ My blood pressure goes up.

____ I lose my breath or it becomes uneven.

BODY SIGNS

____ I get headaches.

____ My back hurts.

_____ Certain muscles tighten and stiffen.
_____ Certain muscles begin to twitch.
_____ I stutter or stammer.
_____ I can't stay in one place very long.
_____ My hands shake.
_____ My vision gets bad.

These SOS signals from your body can let you know something needs your attention. Don't panic when the signals appear. Ask yourself, "What's going on?"

Another part of awareness is being able to monitor the accumulative effects of change in our lives.

Two researchers at the University of Washington, Drs. Holmes and Rahe, have developed a rating scale to examine the connection between major life events and illness or injury. Called the Social Readjustment Rating Scale, or Life Change Scale, this tool has been useful in relating the occurrence of forty-three life events to the likelihood of physical illness.

For example, should you accumulate 150 points or less on the scale within a one-year period, there is a 33 percent probability that you will contract a significant illness or suffer an accident within the next two years. This is the normal amount of risk.

Between 150 and 300 points, your chances rise to about 50-50 that you will have an illness or accident.

With a score of 300 points or more, the chances climb to 90 percent. Make sure your health insurance is paid up if your score is this high! Too much life change over a short period of time is highly related to illness. The greater the amount of life change, the more serious the illness. [2]

A copy of the Life Change Scale is reproduced on pages 50-51. Determine your own score. You may have seen this scale before and evaluated your situation at that time. Your life has probably changed, so it will be helpful to get a current assessment.

Check the events that have occurred in your life over the past year. If the same type of event occurred more than once, be sure to multiply the point value by the number of times the life change event occurred. For example, if you moved three times in the past year, you have accumulated 60 points for those changes (3 x 20).

LIFE CHANGE SCALE[3]

Rank		Mean Value	Score
1	Death of spouse	100	_____
2	Divorce	73	_____
3	Marital separation	65	_____
4	Jail term	63	_____
5	Death of close family member	63	_____
6	Personal injury or illness	53	_____
7	Marriage	50	_____
8	Fired at work	47	_____
9	Marital reconciliation	45	_____
10	Retirement	45	_____
11	Change in health of family member	44	_____
12	Pregnancy	40	_____
13	Sex difficulties	39	_____
14	Gain new family member	39	_____
15	Business readjustment	39	_____
16	Change in financial state	38	_____
17	Death of close friend	37	_____
18	Change to different line of work	36	_____
19	Change in number of arguments with spouse	35	_____
20	Mortgage over $50,000	31	_____
21	Foreclosure of mortgage or loan	30	_____
22	Change in responsibilities at work	29	_____
23	Son or daughter leaving home	29	_____
24	Trouble with in-laws	29	_____
25	Outstanding personal achievement	28	_____
26	Wife begins or stops work	26	_____
27	Begin or end school	26	_____
28	Change in living conditions	25	_____
29	Revision of personal habits	24	_____
30	Trouble with boss	23	_____
31	Change in work hours or conditions	20	_____

32	Change in residence	20	_____
33	Change in schools	20	_____
34	Change in recreation	19	_____
35	Change in church activities	19	_____
36	Change in social activities	18	_____
37	Mortgage or loan less than $50,000	17	_____
38	Change in sleeping habits	16	_____
39	Change in number of family get-togethers	15	_____
40	'Change in eating habits	15	_____
41	Vacation	13	_____
42	Christmas	12	_____
43	Minor violations of the law	11	_____
		Total	_____

Does your score suggest a lot of change in your life? Change is not something we can avoid even if we wanted to. However, change is not random. We do have control over many things that happen. We can choose whether or when to marry, buy a house, or have a family. We can predict some of the future, and to that degree we can learn to order our lives.

It's important to consider the consequences of the changes we make. We need to regulate, to the degree we can, the occurrence of voluntary changes to keep our yearly life change score out of the critical zone.

● *Step 2—Coping with stress.* Now the question arises, "I'm painfully aware that I have 342 stress points. What shall I do?" The urge may be to check into the closest hospital and wait for illness to strike.

There is an alternative. Remember the figures about the stress test. If a person accumulates more than 300 points, there is a 90 per cent chance of physical problems. Another way of looking at that statistic is to observe one person out of ten does *not* have any physical problems. We want to know how that one person in ten avoids major problems, even though he or she has faced as much stress as anyone. While we may not easily change many of life's stressful situations, we can always be ready to improve the way we adapt.

With this perspective in mind, let's examine Elijah's life to see if we can learn some important lessons about coping with stress.

Elijah lived during the reign of evil King Ahab. Through the influence of Ahab's wife, Jezebel, the worship of Baal was prevalent. Handing down God's judgment on Ahab's idolatry, Elijah made himself quite unpopular with the king by predicting that a serious drought and famine would strike the land. Elijah then spent three and a half years in the desert.

On his return, Elijah confronted Ahab with the futility of worshiping Baal. In fact, Elijah proposed an Old Testament Super Bowl to demonstrate who was the one true God. It seemed a little one-sided—450 prophets of Baal versus one man of God.

Each side prepared a sacrifice and prayed for fire to consume the altar. Only the God of Elijah responded with fire, and the people responded in belief (1 Kings 18:39).

After doing away with the prophets of Baal, Elijah sent Ahab home and went to the mountaintop to pray for rain. After praying, Elijah "girded up his loins" and outran Ahab back to Jezreel.

Jezebel was not very happy with these events. She threatened to kill Elijah. So he had to make a hasty retreat out of town.

The next scene finds Elijah in the desert again. Alone, and tired from all that running, Elijah is sitting under a scrawny little juniper tree. He is in the depths of depression. He wishes he were dead.

I'm not so sure you or I would have felt any better. Out of curiosity, I added up all the stress points in this period of Elijah's life. The total was 833! No wonder he was depressed!

The evidence is clear. Elijah experienced extreme stress. Even though we find Elijah at a very low point as he sits under the juniper tree, he later receives help from God and continues to serve.

Several lessons from Elijah's life can help us join that one person in ten who meets stress, but comes out as victor not victim. First . . .

GOD IS NO STRANGER TO STRESS. Stress did not originate in the twentieth century. Look at Elijah 550 years before Christ. No matter which way he turned, it seemed hopeless. Jezebel, out to chop off his head, on one side, and the forbidding, barren desert on the other. There was almost certain death either way.

The psalmist captured this predicament as well as its solution when he wrote, "God is our refuge and strength, an ever present help in trouble" (Ps. 46:1).

The Hebrew word for *trouble* in that verse means being in a narrow, tight place; to be constricted, distressed, and cramped.[4] Another way of putting it would be, "Between a rock and a hard place," or "Between the devil and the deep blue sea."

This is a good way to describe both Elijah's situation and our own. No matter what we do, it seems we are trapped. There is nowhere to turn and we are quickly running out of resources and ideas.

Elijah at this time was depressed and disillusioned. His thinking was very negative. He believed all of his efforts had been wasted and that he was a total failure (1 Kings 19:4).

But Elijah's story wasn't finished yet and neither is ours. Solomon declared, "There is nothing new under the sun," (Ecc. 1:9), and this includes stress. No matter how severe and frustrating a situation looks, God has been there before. He has seen it all. He created the laws of the universe, and those same laws affect our stress. We may not understand them all, but God does. And surely the One that makes the rules ought to be able to help us out of any bind we create for ourselves. In other words, there's hope!

The second lesson . . .

THERE ARE NO LIMITS TO GOD'S POWER. The prophets of Baal prayed and prayed. It didn't do any good. Elijah prayed and God answered. He burned up everything—the sacrifice, stones, water, and the dust around the altar.

God's power is able to overcome any stressor imaginable! There are no restrictions. *All* things are possible with God. Not most or many, but *all*.

To believe in God's unending power has important implications for dealing with stress. We must be aware of the natural human reaction to a threatening situation. When under stress, a person reacts not only to the reality of a stressful event, but also to the perceived threat of that situation.

More than three quarters of our stress is not derived from an actual physical danger, but from imagined threats in our lives. If we *feel* unable to deal with a situation, we are more likely to see it as a high-threat event. And the more threatened we feel, the more profound will be the burden of the stress.

Many people have the ability to give a speech, sing a solo, teach a class, or sell a product. But because of their lack of confidence, they refuse to try. In their own minds, the threat of failure is too great.

Their own perception, however inaccurate, is menacing enough to keep them from taking a chance.

Because of this rule, called the *perception of threat principle*, the Christian approach to stress is radically different. We are not left to our own resources. God is for us (Rom. 8:31), and this knowledge can make a big difference in our willingness to deal with stress. We can walk through the dark valley of death and not be afraid (Ps. 23:4).

The power of God is absolute. "Nothing is too hard for you," exclaimed Jeremiah (Jer. 32:17b). "With man this is impossible, but not with God; all things are possible with God," said Christ to His disciples (Mark 10:27).

Lesson three . . .

WE CAN'T EARN GOD'S HELP. The prophets of Baal prayed and cried to their god. They even cut themselves and went into a mad frenzy to earn Baal's response. This went on for hours, but to no avail. Baal didn't answer.

Elijah, on the other hand, simply prayed to God: "Answer me, O Lord, answer me" (1 Kings 18:37).

God answered Elijah's prayer. It was not because Elijah had earned God's assistance, but because it was God's will to answer.

God's power is not dependent on our help. Thank goodness. It would surely put a limitation on things if God needed our assistance.

"Not that we are competent to claim anything for ourselves, but our competence comes from God" (2 Cor. 3:5).

The grace of God is absolutely free (Rom. 3:24). We don't earn His acceptance or love on the basis of our deeds or actions, but by simple belief in the person of Jesus Christ (Titus 3:5-7).

Elijah acknowledged the God of Israel. God answered Elijah's prayer, not on the basis of his good works, but because of his faith and belief.

The lesson here is to trust and relax in God's wisdom. I learned a lesson in relaxation while taking a trampoline phys. ed. class in college. We were learning to do flips. Things progressed fairly well until I landed crooked and hurt my back. After taking it easy for a few days, I tried to work back into some simple routines. But since the slight injury, a simple drop from a standing position to my stomach was difficult. I was tightening up. Rather than relaxing my back and arm muscles as I hit the surface of the trampoline, I tensed them. That just compounded the problem. The more I tightened up, the harder it became. The only way to conquer the problem was to let go of my fear, concentrate on relaxing, and trust the techniques I had learned.

In the same way, we must learn to let go and let God take control. We must make the best decision we can in regard to our stressful situations. To do that, we need to seek God's help and direction. And then learn to relax. We can't earn God's help. He just wants a trusting heart.

Lesson four . . .

GOD'S HELP IS IMMEDIATELY AVAILABLE. God doesn't say, "Just a minute, I have another priority to take care of first."

God answered Elijah's prayers immediately. The fire came down and consumed the sacrifice as soon as he finished praying. The prophets of Baal had tried for more than three hours. Of course, they were praying to the wrong source.

Later, Elijah was alone in the desert, tired, hungry and discouraged. We see that God took immediate care of his needs. Elijah took a nap and God provided food and water. It must have been a high-energy snack because Elijah lasted forty days on the strength of that food! (1 Kings 19:8)

Some time ago, the organization where I work purchased a new computerized phone system. Though the kinks were eventually worked out, it was difficult to complete phone calls for the first several weeks. During that time a friend tried repeatedly to get through to me. When he finally did make contact, his first statement was, "Grant, God is a whole lot easier to get hold of than you are!" He was right. God is always accessible.

"But hold on a minute," you say. "I have prayed to God and not received a quick response. What do you mean, God doesn't make us wait?"

The problem is threefold. First, God promises to supply our needs, not our wants. God gives us what is best for our growth and maturity, not necessarily what we've asked for.

Second, we don't have God's perspective. For example, we don't see how an apparent delay on God's part is an occasion for teaching us patience.

A friend of mine resigned his job several years ago thinking he had a definite position at another institution. Suddenly, funding problems arose and he was told the new job was unavailable. By then his former job had been filled by someone else and his home had been sold. An entire year passed before a permanent position and residence were found, a year of much prayer and searching for God's will as well as one of questioning and discouragement.

I asked about the turn of events and how he felt. He replied he would never want to repeat that year of struggle, but he and his wife wouldn't trade the experience and maturity gained for anything in the world. While they didn't relish the idea of going through it again, they had learned a dependency on God that they might not have acquired otherwise.

When we pray, God is immediately available, but we may not be fully aware of exactly how He is going to answer that prayer. We have to believe Christ's words from the Sermon on the Mount: "Ask and it will be given to you" (Matt. 7:7).

Third, we must abide in Christ as a condition for answers to our prayers (John 15:7). This means we must keep His commandments (John 15:10) and be obedient. Elijah did what God told him to do. Even after collapsing in a depressed heap in the desert, Elijah was obedient. After receiving nourishment, Elijah traveled to Mount Horeb, where God instructed him to anoint two new kings and Elisha as his replacement (1 Kings 19:8-16). And Elijah did just as God commanded.

We can't expect God to answer our prayers if we aren't obedient. Jonah found himself in the belly of a great fish because he tried to run away from God. God had asked Jonah to go to Nineveh and preach against its wickedness. Jonah didn't like the idea and tried to flee. His disobedience lead to his predicament (Jonah 1:1-17).

If we find ourselves having difficulty with stress, despite our prayers, we must make sure we are acting in obedience to the Lord.

Finally, a fifth lesson . . .

WE MUST DEPEND ON GOD. We end our discussion of Elijah, still "alone" in the desert. There was no one to turn to but God. And God was there every time, providing food and water, hearing his concerns, and giving new direction.

How many times have we been in a desert situation of our lives and only out of desperation did we turn toward God? Many of us seem reluctant to admit our entire life force comes from our Creator

(2 Cor. 3:5; 4:7). We are in a struggle to prove our own superiority and independence.

In contrast, one of the basic lessons that God would have us learn from the thorn of stress is to be dependent on Him. God wants us to look to Him for strength and power rather than to our own efforts.

When stressors present themselves, we need to believe and remember we are not alone. It's a golden opportunity to see our human limitations and the power of God. Our masks of self-confidence and self-sufficiency can then be replaced by God's caring and loving presence.

This lesson might best be illustrated by an incident involving my son Bryce. One evening he came running up the stairs from the shop where he had been working on his bicycle. He was struggling with a flat tire. Bryce fussed with the tools, inner tube, and pump for quite a while. He took it about as far as his skill would allow. Finally, in frustration, he came up and said, "Dad, I don't know what I am doing. Will you help?"

Sometimes we wait too long to ask for God's help. Emotions and lives may be damaged before we seek His aid. How much better it would be if we would learn to depend on and trust our God from the start, not as a last resort.

Stress can be either a time of trauma or growth. If we are to learn to handle stress as Elijah did, we must claim the promise of the psalmist: "The Lord is my light and my salvation—whom shall I fear? The Lord is the stronghold of my life—of whom shall I be afraid"? (Ps. 27:1)

FIVE

*"Carry each other's
burdens"*
(Gal. 6:2).

THE GIFT
OF DEPRESSION

People may say, "You just don't seem like your old self. Anything wrong?"

You're having difficulty getting out of bed in the morning; decisions are difficult; it's hard to concentrate. Apathy and discouragement are your prevailing feelings.

Sleeping problems—too much or too little, sexual disinterest, pessimism, social isolation, irritability, lethargy, and feelings of hopelessness and gloom characterize your life.

The doctor says there's nothing wrong with you physically, but headaches, stomach problems, backaches, or allergies seem to plague you constantly.

These are signs of depression. It's the most frequent emotional problem in our society. Depression is the "common cold" of the mental health field. Almost everybody has had at least a touch of it.

A National Institute of Mental Health study revealed that 75 percent of all psychiatric hospitalizations were for depression. In any given year, it is estimated that 15 percent of all the adults between ages eighteen and seventy-four may suffer significant problems with depression. Perhaps one of every eight individuals in the United States will experience depression in his or her lifetime. This amounts to between four and eight million people who are depressed to the extent they cannot effectively function at their work or home, or must find some kind of treatment.[1]

No one is immune to depression—not even Christians. And it's not new. Sorrow, discouragement, and depression are found again and again in the pages of Scripture:

"The Lord is close to the brokenhearted and saves those who are crushed in spirit" (Ps. 34:18).

"O Jehovah, God of my salvation, I have wept before You day and night. Now hear my prayers; oh, listen to my cry, for my life is full of troubles, and death draws near. They say my life is ebbing out—a hopeless case. You have thrust me down to the darkest depths. Your wrath lies heavy on me; wave after wave engulfs me" (Ps. 88:1-4, 6-7, TLB).

Other examples of depression can be found in the lives of Moses (Num. 11:10-16); David (2 Sam. 12:1-17); Elijah (1 Kings 19:1-8); and Jonah (Jonah 4:1-11).

LESSONS FROM DEPRESSION

Depression is no doubt a common and disabling occurrence. On the other hand, depression can be a vehicle for positive change. It may seem like a contradiction to title this chapter "The Gift of Depression," but there are definite reasons why depression can be profitable.

A complete discussion of the treatment of depression would have to include causative factors responsible for the illness. I will not describe the different sources or solutions for depression. Many good books speak to those issues. Here we'll only look at the four lessons that God might teach us within depression, without getting into such detail. To begin . . .

● *Depression is not a sin.* Depression is threatening. As Christians, we may believe that we shouldn't get depressed. We may believe there is sin in our lives or failure to live up to God's expectations. Though this may certainly be the case, depression itself is not a sin.

If depression were a sin, Jesus would have sinned. Christ wept in response to the death of His friend Lazarus (John 11:35). He wept over Jerusalem as He foresaw the destruction of the city which had rejected Him (Luke 19:41).

Jesus was even more distraught in the Garden of Gethsemane. "He took Peter and the two sons of Zebedee along with Him, and He began to be sorrowful and troubled. Then He said to them, 'My soul is overwhelmed with sorrow to the point of death. Stay here and keep watch with Me' " (Matt. 26:37-38). The Lord's feelings are clearly those of depression. But we also know Jesus was without sin (1 Peter 2:22), so it is possible to experience this feeling without necessarily associating it with sinful behavior.

Depression can be a very natural response to grief, loss, confusion, competition, or stress. Viewed as a signal, we should pay attention to our depression. But we should not always assume sin is the cause.

Depression can certainly occur as a result of sin. King Saul tried to kill David due to feelings of frustration, envy, and anger. His depression was a result of poor choices and sinful behavior (1 Sam. 18).

Jonah is another example of depression resulting from sin. He didn't agree with God's willingness to forgive the people of Nineveh; he wanted the city destroyed instead. Jonah tried to run away from God, but three days in the tummy of a whale slowed him down a bit.

Jonah then reacted to God's mercy with sinful anger. He stomped off to the outskirts of Nineveh and had a temper tantrum. He was still hoping the city would be destroyed.

As a result of his anger toward God, Jonah experienced depression. "Now, O Lord, take away my life, for it is better for me to die than to live" (Jonah 4:3).

The sins of prejudice, hatred, and anger toward God triggered Jonah's depression. The depression was not the sin. It was an emotional response to poor choices by Jonah.

Far from representing sin, depression can be a plateau period of rest or regeneration. Christ withdrew to the desert because He and the disciples needed time away from the crowds (Mark 6:31-32). They weren't depressed in the usual sense, but they did need a quiet place to be alone and get some rest (Mark 7:24; Luke 9:10). The desire to be alone is interpreted by some as a mild depression. In reality, it may be a legitimate time to wind down.

After accomplishing a major goal such as a promotion, athletic championship, or graduation, many people experience a letdown or mild depression. After completing my doctorate in psychology, I felt uneasy and apathetic for about six months. Somehow there just had to be another paper to complete or another exam to take. Most of the previous twenty years had been spent in education—from grade school to graduate school. Course requirements were second nature to me. Their absence left me apprehensive.

My new job as a clinical professor at the university kept me busy during the day, but I spent many wasted evening hours sleeping on the couch. I'd accomplished a major goal in my life, but I was not prepared for the letdown that followed.

My feelings of apathy and depression were not sin. Those feelings were a natural emotional response to a long, hard expenditure of effort. I needed a period of rest and contemplation before fully delving into the next stages of my life.

Moses had a similar, more dramatic experience. He had talked to God face to face (Ex. 33:11). It was a literal mountaintop experience! Then the reality of dealing with the complaining Children of Israel hit home. Moses' response was, "Where am I supposed to get meat for all these people? For they weep to me saying, 'Give us meat!' I can't carry this nation by myself! The load is far too heavy! If you are going to treat me like this, please kill me right now; it will be a kindness! Let me out of this impossible situation!" (Num. 11:13-15, TLB)

We shouldn't panic at the first signs of depression and immediately assume the presence of sin. God might be telling us we need to slow down and relax. We may need a time of reduced activity to adjust our priorities or to set new goals.

Depression can also result from physical sources outside our control. A forty-two year old woman came to me with all the signs of depression. There were a number of problem areas in her family, but I was curious about her medical status. I requested she get a physical evaluation that included testing of hormone levels. The doctor reported she was suffering severe estrogen deprivation and prescribed immediate injections. She began feeling better in just a few days. No sin was present, just poor body chemistry. It was not a miracle cure. Her other family concerns remained. But at least now she is able to attempt to cope with those problems at full strength.

Improper diet, inadequate sleep, drugs, infections, and glandular disorders can contribute to depression. It is usually not sin, but physiological reactions that account for the depression in these cases.

● *Depression is a warning.* The major purpose of depression is to warn us that something in our system needs attention before more serious consequences occur. It can be like a fire alarm ringing to tell us something inside is overheating. In this way depression is a gift.

With this perspective, we can thank God for the depression. What we are saying is, "Thank You, Lord, for letting me know something is wrong. Now tell me what I need to do to get things back in harmony."

Remember Kathy from chapter 1? She is an example of the body's warning system being used to bring about beneficial changes. The crying spells, body pains, and depression caused her to seek help. With help, she learned her emotional and spiritual systems were out of balance. When improvements were made, Kathy was able to see how her depression caused her to grow. Maturity came out of misery.

Jonah's depression was a result of his disobedience and anger against God. Elijah's depression signaled the presence of large amounts of stress. Moses' depression represented overwhelming job pressure.

Jeremiah also dealt with extreme depths of depression. Because of his heavyheartedness, he is called the Weeping Prophet. Though reluctant to speak, Jeremiah began his ministry at about age twenty. A sensitive and sympathetic person by nature, he was asked by God to deliver a very stern message of judgment. More than once he wanted to quit. Yet for more than forty years, he faithfully proclaimed God's verdict on godless Judah. All the while he endured opposition, beatings, and jail.

No wonder Jeremiah expressed these feelings: "Alas, my mother, that you gave me birth, a man with whom the whole land strives and contends! I have never lent nor borrowed, yet everyone curses me" (Jer. 15:10).

"Cursed be the day I was born! May the day my mother bore me not be blessed! . . . Why did I ever come out of the womb to see trouble and sorrow and to end my days in shame?" (Jer. 20:14, 18)

"Since my people are crushed, I am crushed; I mourn, and horror grips me" (Jer. 8:21).

Jeremiah's mournfulness signaled several sources of concern, but the basic cause of his depression was rejection. His family turned against him (Jer. 12:6). He could not marry and have his own children (Jer. 16:2). He couldn't socialize with his own people, so he lived an isolated life (Jer. 16:8).

We see his rejection in these words, "O Lord, You deceived me, and I was deceived . . . I am ridiculed all day long; everyone mocks me . . . So the word of the Lord has brought me insult and reproach all day long" (Jer. 20:7-8).

Fortunately, Jeremiah turned to God for help and direction, knowing his own resources were depleted. And help did come! God brought changes in Jeremiah's thinking which allowed him to reaffirm God's providence.

Once the alarm has sounded and we find the fire's source, something must be done to put out the flames. It doesn't do any good to stand around wringing our hands and bemoaning the destruction taking place. We must take action!

• *Depression demands change.* A teachable moment occurs when we realize our depression can be used to make changes that will bring about growth. Those changes need to be appropriate to the problem at hand. Superficial first aid won't do. A garden hose applied to a roaring inferno will not get the job done.

Remember the old wall plaque—"Smile, things could be worse. So I smiled. And sure enough, things got worse!" Or how about the one that says, "The light at the end of the tunnel is the headlamp of an oncoming train!"

Neither shallow optimism nor fatalistic pessimism is the appropriate change for depression.

Jeremiah made the right changes. First, he told God the exact nature of his problem—he was depressed, felt rejected by his people, and thought God had abandoned him.

We need to be equally honest and aware. It's important to admit we are down. Denying our feelings only makes the problem worse. Second, Jeremiah challenged his feelings of rejection by reviewing and reacknowledging the fact of God's total and continual acceptance. "Yet this I call to mind and therefore I have hope: Because of the Lord's great love we are not consumed, for His compassions never fail. They are new every morning; great is Your faithfulness" (Lam. 3:21-23).

Jeremiah dealt with his feelings of rejection by reminding himself of his acceptance by God. "When Your words came, I ate them; they were my joy and my heart's delight, for I bear Your name, O Lord God Almighty" (Jer. 15:16). What better acceptance is there than to be called by and identified with God Himself!

The third step in the change process came with the correction in

Jeremiah's thinking. Jeremiah had allowed his emotions to take control. He had lost perspective of God's purpose for his life. He likened God to an empty stream, incapable of quenching his thirst. He felt God had failed him.

God dealt clearly with Jeremiah's bad attitude. " 'If you repent, I will restore you that you may serve Me; if you utter worthy, not worthless words, you will be My spokesman. For I am with you to rescue and save you,' declares the Lord" (Jer. 15:19-20).

Depression often comes from illogical or incorrect thinking. Jeremiah's did. He thought God had deserted him. God corrected that assumption. God was very much in control. And while Jeremiah had met with earthly rejection, God promised He would deliver him.

It is important to keep our mind focused on worthwhile and true thoughts as we make the changes necessary to respond to our depression (Phil. 4:8).

DEPRESSION CAN TEACH US HOW TO RECEIVE

Another lesson in depression is learning how to receive love and support from those who care for us.

For many, this is a difficult lesson to learn. The major problem is that we don't know how to receive. Think of our typical reaction when someone compliments us. We tend to stutter, stammer, and avoid eye contact. We quickly qualify or make excuses for our success. "Oh, I found it on the sale rack." Or, "It's just something I threw together. I'm sure you could do better."

We seem to feel it's inappropriate to simply accept the fact the other person liked what we accomplished.

Yes, we are told to bear one another's burdens (Gal. 6:2). Equally important, however, is our need to experience the growth that comes from being nurtured, uplifted, and sustained by fellow believers.

A good receiver will make a better giver the next time around. It isn't possible to empathize with someone else's burden unless we have allowed someone to share our burdens. Having received, we are able to give in a more sensitive manner.

When we experience the agony of depression, we have greater empathy for the feelings of frustration and helplessness in the lives of others. With the benefit of this shared experience, we are less likely to respond to their hurt with empty platitudes or clichés. A bond is established by having traveled the same road.

Many helpful support groups have been established on the basis of common backgrounds or common pain. For example, Alcoholics Anonymous seems to be successful because all the members have shared the struggle with excessive drinking. Everyone who attends knows the agony of being out of control. As a result, they can be effective helpers for each other.

Jesus provided us with an example of gracious receiving. While eating dinner in the home of Simon the leper, a woman entered with a jar of expensive perfume and proceeded to pour the fine ointment on Jesus' head. The disciples became very upset about the waste of money this act of giving involved (Mark 14:3-9).

Jesus replied, "She has done a beautiful thing to Me" (v. 6). Christ found it appropriate to accept the gift. We can follow His example, knowing we are bringing joy and encouragement to the one who gives, as well as receiving the benefit of the gift.

By denying our problems and not allowing others to help us, we are denying God a chance to work through the giftedness and mercifulness of His servants. If a friend comes to us with a sincere desire to support us in our depression and we react by pretending everything is fine, we may be frustrating his or her act of obedience to God. It's important to allow others to use their gifts on our behalf. Unity of the body of believers is enhanced by those who receive (Rom. 12:5-6; 1 Cor. 10:17).

Stop and think about the implications of the command to bear one another's burdens. You need both a bearer and a bearee. Everyone can't be burden-free all the time. Of course, this doesn't mean we should become depressed just so we can give the burden bearers something to do! I am merely suggesting God doesn't expect us to always be on the giving end of things. When we hurt, it's just fine with God if we accept the love and compassion of those who care about us.

We are not to be dependent on others any longer than necessary. Nor should we aspire to be weak or depressed. But when we do find ourselves overwhelmed by discouragement, pessimism, and melancholy, we should give ourselves permission to receive gifts of mercy.

My father, L.B. Martin, died of cancer in 1965. "L.B.", as he was called, was an independent man. Dad was a successful farmer in southern Idaho and active in his community and state. He was involved in both state and national farm-related legislation, and stepped down from his position as president of the Idaho State Farm Bureau Federation and as member of the National Farm Bureau Board only a short time before his death.

Dad wasn't a talker; he was a doer. He was the resource other people in the community came to for help. Since he kept his farm machinery in good condition, other farmers sometimes asked to borrow his equipment when theirs broke down. Because of his success, neighboring farms would consult L.B. about the best crop rotation, fertilizer usage, and irrigation schedules. Dad would always share what he knew, and studied to know more.

At age forty-four, Dad was diagnosed with inoperable pancreatic cancer. The first symptoms occurred around Thanksgiving, the cancer was discovered during the winter, and Dad was gone by early April.

Dad's initial reaction was understandable. He tried to be optimistic. He joked about taking a vacation but stated his intentions to resume his farming activities as soon as possible. He knew all the time that unless God intervened he would not survive the cancer's onslaught.

Dad was not used to being helpless. He preferred to do things himself. If there was a piece of machinery to be welded, he welded it; if there was a problem to be solved, he had the tenacity and skills to solve it. He couldn't, however, fix the cancer in his abdomen. It was very uncomfortable for him to suddenly become dependent.

Dad was usually the one who gave. He did not like being on the receiving end of things. A positive change occurred when Dad was able to accept the love, affection, affirmation, and concern of the many friends and relatives who visited him. Though he didn't talk about it much, Dad knew he was facing death. He knew he was dependent not only on the medical resources, but also on the support of the family, friends, and community members who loved him. It took a lot of honesty and courage to admit he was not able to control the growth of the cancer as he had been able to control the growth of sugar beets or corn. It took God's presence to help Dad surrender emotionally and accept the unconditional love of his church and community.

Dad shared his faith and confidence with all who visited him, whether a state congressman or a neighboring farmhand. His ability to retain a sense of humor and perspective left an indelible mark and testimony on all those who knew him.

Dad's memorial service was a time of celebration. In his relatively short life, he'd given much to many. In his dignity, manner of faith, and courage, he gave even in his death. Yet as I look back on that time, the greatest blessing was Dad's ability to receive.

The German word for *depression* means "the courage to be heavy-hearted" or "the courage to live with that which is difficult." Though depression is a frequent visitor in the lives of many of us, it can still be thought of as a gift. The gift is paradoxical. Depression brings sorrow and discouragement. But it can also be a helpful teacher.

THE DARK NIGHT OF THE SOUL

Another lesson is possible in an experience that seems close to depression in its symptoms, but not in its source. The experience of the "dark night of the soul" is a common theme in mystical literature. St. John of the Cross (1542-1591) describes with great vividness the soul's bereftness during periods of struggle to recapture the lost sense of God's nearness.

The common quality in descriptions of the "dark night" is a frustrated quest for God's presence. One who experienced a meaningful relationship with God finds to his dismay that he seems further from God than before despite his obedience. This deprivation throws the emotions into confusion, turmoil, and deep distress.

It's the kind of spiritual desert described in Isaiah 50:10—"Who among you fears the Lord and obeys the word of His servant? Let him who walks in the dark, who has no light, trust in the name of the Lord and rely on his God."

The following symptoms of the "dark night" are described by various authors:

Feelings of dryness and depression.
A sense of loss.
Spiritual apathy.
Sensory and spiritual appetites seem dead or asleep.
Little or no imagination or creativity.
Loss of memory or lack of comprehension, particularly of spiritual things.

The will is constrained. Feelings of bondage or fear
of engaging in any venture of faith.
Bible reading, sermons, or study groups may fail to
move, excite, or stimulate.[2]

There may be a temptation to blame the pastor or teachers for not
providing any spiritual food for thought, even though others in the
same setting are being fed. There is a sense of loneliness from both
God and man. The soul cries out for human fellowship, but the pain
of the experience makes the sufferer difficult to be around. Generally,
there is a feeling of spiritual impotency, though, for the most part,
yielding to temptation does not occur. Spiritual helplessness seems to
be a dominant theme.[3]
Individuals describe this condition in several ways:

I prayed constantly for help, but it seemed of no avail.
Instead of prayer bringing comfort, it brought me pain. I
felt that I had forever forfeited the right to God's mercy, so
deep was the burden of guilt and self-condemnation upon
my soul.

* * *

I tried to pray but without avail. The God I trusted I could
not find in my extremity. Why?

* * *

What was my state of mind in this "black night of the
soul"? There was ever and again the wish to be dead. If I
could just cease to exist! But that was the rub. I believed
that dying did not end it all. I felt resentment that it did
not.

Toward those few good people who gave me their ut-
most in precious friendship, I would cry out at times wish-
ing to God that they had been spared the knowledge of
me, for I was so sure that in the end I could bring them
only pain.

I hungered to know God, to have fellowship with Him.
But it seemed that I could know Him only through the
experience of others, only through hearsay. Internally I
lived in hell though I walked the earth.

But I'd go through it all again, if need be, for the glory that has come to me because I have found Him who is indeed the Light of Life.

* * *

The "turning point" in my recovery came when I ceased regretting the past, ceased pitying myself, and asked only for God and His presence and His power in my life. I know what it means to "hunger and thirst after righteousness" and then to experience the joy of being filled.[4]

It's important to separate this "dark night" experience from depression described earlier, even though there are many similarities in symptoms. The distinguishing feature is the lack of any psychological mechanism such as internalized anger, low self-esteem, or inappropriate expectations prior to the onset of the experience.

The purpose of the "dark night of the soul" from God's point of view is not to afflict or punish us, but to set us free from what we believed were spiritual necessities.[5] It seems to be a divine appointment to draw closer to God and to be singularly and exclusively focused on our relationship to Him.

A friend of mine identified the "dark night" as part of her spiritual pilgrimage. Pam didn't know what to call it at the time, but she was familiar with its components, symptoms, and outcome. At one point, Pam felt the church was no longer meeting her needs. Prayer was not meaningful and hymns had lost their impact. She began to blame her husband, family, and church fellowship for not being supportive or caring.

Because of the experience, Pam eventually drew closer to God. She had to. There was nothing or no one else to fall back on. All the religious support systems and crutches had lost their value. While potentially meaningful and good, Pam found that church, sermons, family, and friends were not essential prerequisites for her relationship with God.

Finally, Pam found a new and closer communication with God that was not dependent on anything but her own faith and desire to love Him.

I don't know how common this experience may be. Remember, there is a distinction between a desert experience which is under the

69

authorship of God and those instances of depression which are the result of our own choices, misbelief, or disobedience. Every time you feel a little down, uninspired by a sermon, or apathetic about spiritual things, don't immediately assume you are experiencing a "dark night."

This may be an uncommon experience, and perhaps, like the discipline of fasting, should be private in nature. But there is biblical precedent that this "dark night of the soul" could be another of the treasures out of darkness. If it is, we need to be aware of its potential and be sensitive to its place and purpose in the lives of growing Christians.

SIX

"A man ought to examine himself" (1 Cor. 11:28).

"If anyone thinks he is something when he is nothing, he deceives himself" (Gal. 6:3).

LEARNING TO LOVE WHO WE ARE

Betty is a vivacious woman, married, with two children. Her husband is an honest and faithful provider. He has no bad habits and is usually considerate and kind. But Betty has a problem.

"I want to leave everything and run away," she exclaimed.

"Why do you feel this way?" I asked.

"I don't know why. I just feel I have to get out," she replied through tears of frustration and anxiety.

There had to be reasons for her feelings. So we explored what had happened over the past seventeen years of her marriage.

Betty grew up in a conservative Christian home, lived in a close-knit community, and had gone to a Christian school. She, along with many of her friends, married right after graduating from high school. The pattern continued from there. She tended to follow the values, ideals, and expectations of her family and friends and seldom developed her own.

She had not considered attending college because most of her girlfriends had become homemakers and mothers. Betty possessed many potential talents and abilities, but hadn't developed many of them. Setting goals for herself had never been a priority.

Taking responsibility for decisions about her purpose and ministry in life hadn't concerned Betty. She had very little identity outside of being the wife of Jack, the electronics salesman and church elder.

Things went along fairly smoothly until Betty began working out-

71

side the home. She enjoyed the freedom her work provided. It was satisfying to make new friends at the office. At the same time, Betty felt guilty and confused. She didn't think it was permissible for a Christian wife to find a meaningful identity outside the role of wife and mother. For the first time, she had friends outside her husband's circle of acquaintances. She found delight in receiving a phone call from someone Jack didn't know. Later, guilt feelings would set in.

In her confusion, Betty was tempted to throw away the marriage. It was impossible for her to continue with the dual allegiances she found inside herself. She didn't want to give up the friendships and satisfaction of her work. But the guilt was turning her into a nervous wreck. Betty was at her wits end and leaving seemed the only solution.

THANK GOODNESS FOR PROBLEMS

One of the Beatitudes (Matt. 5:3) paraphrased by Dr. Raymond Cramer reads, "Congratulations when we find ourselves in a difficult situation because satisfying results will follow if certain conditions are met."[1]

The good news does not come because we are poor in spirit or because we are weak. Congratulations are due because there is the possibility of satisfying results if certain conditions are met. One of those conditions is the willingness to work through our problems. We can't run away from life's thorny situations if we want to experience positive results.

We often go to great lengths to avoid dealing with our problems. We take out a second mortgage or increase our credit card spending limits rather than deal with the issue of financial irresponsibility. We blame other people for being difficult to get along with instead of changing our judgmental attitudes.

Life can be a roller coaster. As someone once said, "The average American is one whose daily intake of pep pills balances out his daily quota of tranquilizers so that he can make his weekly trip to the psychiatrist."

Quick solutions are scarce. Pills only change a person's chemistry so life doesn't seem so bleak. Denial only delays the confrontation. Our thorns must eventually be faced.

Betty was ready to examine those "certain conditions that would lead her to satisfying results. She'd arrived at a teachable moment.

While on the verge of giving up her family, she had an opportunity to stop and examine her options.

Betty was in a difficult situation. I empathized with her and assured her she could take advantage of the crisis. There was an alternative to the isolation and restricted identity she experienced.

Betty and her husband needed a marriage model in which Jack could have identity as a salesman and elder and Betty could maintain her role as a receptionist and bookkeeper. In addition to their separate identities, they could also have a mutual identity as husband and wife, parents, and best friends.

Betty concluded it was OK for her and Jack to develop friendships outside their common experiences. This awareness gave new hope and vitality to their relationship. Betty chose not to leave the marriage. In fact, she became more committed to being a loving wife. Some of her social and self-esteem needs were met so Betty had more energy to put into the marriage.

Jack grew to appreciate this new perspective also. Instead of losing, he gained an enthusiastic and creative wife who had more purpose and meaning in her life.

Betty's crisis turned into a growth opportunity. Initially, she believed there was very little meaning and purpose in life. Low self-esteem plagued her. She mistakenly thought her husband was the

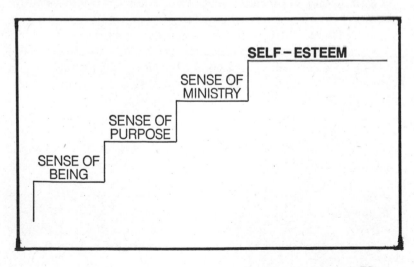

only one who could contribute something important to the community. Betty's frustration led her to examine the accuracy of her self-esteem. By finding she'd made incorrect assumptions, Betty established a new foundation, which became the building block for a healthy and positive self-image.

Poor self-esteem is one of the most common thorns we encounter. Each of us has doubted his ability at one time or another. Even doubt, however, can become an opportunity to affirm who we are and clarify how we fit into the kingdom of God.

Three steps in the process of developing self-esteem are shown in the chart on page 73. Each step builds on the preceding step in the maturing life of a Christian.

STEP 1: SENSE OF BEING

The first element in self-esteem requires coming to an understanding of our fundamental nature. It asks the question, "Who am I?"

An accurate vision of personal possibilities is needed. God has made us whole and complete (2 Cor. 5:17; Col. 3:10). If we can understand and accept ourselves, we will grow toward that essential completeness.

It takes real courage to accept ourselves in our present condition. Knowing that our personalities contain defects and weaknesses, we must still learn to accept ourselves. An internal struggle does exist. We have desires and impulses contrary to our Christian values, but we can't afford to deny the existence of this conflict.

A husband reported to me his affair with a woman at work. He'd told his wife about their relationship and now their marriage was in turmoil. This wasn't the first time he had yielded to sexual temptation. But it was the first time his wife knew.

Several factors contributed to the problem. The first was the husband's extensive denial of feelings. For years he had experienced anger, but didn't express it openly. He was angry about his alcoholic and immoral parents and the instability they caused in his childhood. He felt insecure and inadequate, but had attempted to hide those feelings. As a Christian, he believed he had to suppress *all* his anger *all* the time.

His headaches and lower-back pain took on a different meaning when he realized how his lack of outward expression had caused inner tension. Because he seldom talked about his feelings there was no safety valve to prevent the buildup of frustrations.

He first had to become aware of his nature. That included both the strong and the weak, the thorns and the roses. He then had to accept the entire package. He wouldn't like everything he saw. Improvement was necessary. Acceptance meant he had to be honest about the facts of his condition.

A second aspect of the situation was the wife's unrealistic view of her husband. She had placed him on a pedestal. In her eyes, he could do no wrong. She was blind, however, to the problems this created. First, it denied her an adequate sense of being, identity, and equality. She saw very little value in herself. She was "only" a wife and mother. This idealized perspective of her husband kept her from dealing with herself. He was the standard-bearer. He was the one who had value. Her worth came only by the fact that she was married to this outstanding person.

This woman had refused to come to terms with her own sense of being. Her self-esteem was low, so by further avoiding personal examination, she escaped taking responsibility for herself.

Ignorance is bliss. When we refuse to acknowledge faults, we avoid assuming responsibility for them. Here were two people with low opinions of themselves who were unable to grow because they refused to be honest.

Knowledge of her husband's adultery certainly brought him down from his pedestal in a hurry! He no longer was seen as the all-knowing, unfailing knight in shining armor. The wife responded with understandable anger. Initially, most of that anger was directed at the other woman. Even her anger, however, kept the wife from seeing the heart of the problem. By focusing her anger on the other woman, the wife was resisting the need to make changes in her own life.

Eventually, this couple rebuilt their marriage on a more solid foundation. They reaffirmed their commitment to each other. New channels of communication were established. They gained an improved awareness of themselves as individuals with unique needs, drives, and motives. Though intense pain and scar tissue remained, the situation became an opportunity for growth.

Our sense of being can start with the admission of weakness. We may have to acknowledge the existence of personality defects, social inadequacies, or spiritual failures. It may not be pleasant. But without this insight, growth cannot occur.

The following poem reflects part of the struggle and risk encountered on the road to improved self-esteem.

Crazy? Or Sane?

My brain is so busy
Inside my head,
But yet in my heart
Everything's dead.

My head and my heart
Argue a lot—
My head tries to be
What my heart is not.

My heart is unhappy,
It wants to cry,
It hurts so much
That I want to die.

I need to scream,
I need to cry,
I want to kill
And I don't know why.

I need to be loved
For *all* that I am,
Not only the part
That fits another's plan.

My dearest longing
In this world would be
If my heart and my head
Would start to agree.
                    —Anonymous

All struggles may not be that intense. But congruity between what we know in our heads and how we feel in our hearts must be achieved.

● *Self-love.* Developing a sense of being doesn't stop with the recognition of weakness and inadequacies. The process must move on to an appropriate love of self.

The reason thorns can be stepping-stones to improved self-esteem resides in the fact of God's unconditional love for us (John 3:16; 16:27). It's a major step forward when a person realizes he is loved regardless of his personal failures. We have done nothing to deserve God's love, yet it is freely given (Rom. 3:24). It's very encouraging to know God loves us in spite of our weaknesses.

The first time the Bible mentions self-love is in Leviticus 19:18— "Do not seek revenge or bear a grudge against one of your people, but love your neighbor as yourself. I am the Lord."

Mark 12:29-31 records what Jesus Christ felt to be the most important of all God's commandments. First, to love God; then to love our neighbor as we love ourselves. The rest of our Christian life hinges on our fulfillment of these commandments.

The exhortation to "love our neighbor" is repeated several times in Scripture, but never without the command to love ourselves (Rom. 13:9; Gal. 5:14; James 2:8). God knows that it is important to love ourselves, even though we don't naturally do a very good job of it.

"We don't do a good job of loving ourselves?" you ask. "But I thought part of the problem was we loved ourselves too much."

Our old nature tends to be very selfish and self-absorbed. But that is different from an appropriate love of self. A tendency to be selfish is generally motivated by insecurity and anxiety. We respond to that anxiety by trying to control the world around us. It is because we *don't* love ourselves that we act in selfish and immature ways.

A person who accepts and loves himself is more likely to be relaxed and content with his situation in life. Someone who wants everything his way is trying to cover up an intense feeling of insecurity. If the self-centered person really loved himself, he wouldn't need to work so hard to prove his worth.

The one who accepts his personhood, who knows his strengths and weaknesses, and who can affirm himself as God affirms him has nothing to prove. Therefore, the fact that selfishness is present in our lives does not argue against the need to learn to love ourselves.

It is a *fact* that God loves us unconditionally. We are fearfully and wonderfully made (Ps. 139:13-16). We are the product of God's workmanship (Eph. 2:10). We are created in His image (Gen. 1:26). Furthermore, God likes what He sees in us (Gen. 1:31). He didn't take a look, see some imperfections, and say, "Oops, I'd better try again."

God values us enough that He seeks our worship (John 4:23). Christ, His Son, accepts us as we are, with no strings attached (John 6:37). We are precious in God's eyes (Isa. 43:4). We are important enough to God that He allowed the spilling of the blood of His Son, Jesus Christ, for our benefit (1 Peter 1:18-19).

Furthermore, we have been adopted by God and made sons and daughters equal to Jesus Christ! (Rom. 8:14-17)

These are the facts of our value and importance to God. To assist in developing our sense of being, we must *know* these facts.

The next crucial step is *accepting* the love God has given to us. For many, it is difficult to simply receive His gift. They try to earn God's love by being extra good. Others try to qualify by suffering pain and doing penance. The truth is, all we have to do is accept what is freely given.

PARENTS TEACH CHILDREN HOW TO RECEIVE GOD'S LOVE

All of us must learn to receive God's love. It doesn't come naturally. We are able to love only because God first loved us (1 John 4:19).

Early family experiences strongly influence the ease or difficulty with which children are able to accept God's love.

I recall a seventeen-year-old girl who had a stormy relationship with her father. They were constantly bickering, arguing, and criticizing. Because of this, she had a difficult time seeing her Heavenly Father as a loving, caring God. Her father image was a negative, critical, argumentative person who looked for faults and expressed disapproval.

This poor relationship with her father did not excuse her from the accountability for making a choice about God's gift of unconditional love. Her poor relationship with her earthly father, however, certainly made it more difficult to accept the love of her Heavenly Father.

A legacy is anything handed down from an ancestor to a descendant. Families pass on many characteristics and qualities to their children. Two of the most important legacies passed from parents to children are the spiritual and the emotional. These are far more enduring than the family name, stocks, bonds, or large estates.

• *Spiritual legacy.* The spiritual legacy is the example and instruction by parents that introduces children to the Good News of salvation. The importance of developing a personal relationship to Jesus Christ is the basic component of this family tradition. This is accomplished by direct instruction and by "walking our talk" before our children (Deut. 6:5-9).

The Bible affirms the parents' role in sharing this spiritual legacy— "Train a child in the way he should go, and when he is old he will not turn from it" (Prov. 22:6). Because of our sinful nature and free will, this verse is not an ironclad guarantee our children will eventually have a personal relationship to Christ, but it does suggest parental teaching is of vital importance for influencing their choices.

• *Emotional legacy.* The emotional legacy also involves contributions from both parents. Many of the first impressions of life center around the mother-child relationship. Warmth and love must be conveyed by Mother to the child to ensure healthy development. Babies are highly dependent on their mothers for safety and nourishment needs during the early years. The influence of the father usually comes into affect somewhat later, but his legacy is just as important.

The following statement from a book chapter entitled "A Man and His Authority" by my friend and colleague, Dr. James Dobson, emphasizes this point.

> American men have experienced a severe crisis of identity in recent years, similar to the confusion that their wives have encountered. It has been brought on by persistent challenges to everything traditionally masculine, just as the women's movement has mocked traditionally female behavior and mores. Masculine leadership, especially, has been ridiculed as "macho" and invariably self-serving. But the purpose of this chapter has been to reaffirm the importance of authority in a family—first, in the provision of gentle direction and guidance, and second, in raising healthy children. Both objectives appear to be part of the Creator's blueprint for a successful home.[2]

The contribution of fathers to the emotional development of their children has been underemphasized. Fathers have a significant influence in how children will be able to understand and deal with feelings in an open manner. Fathers who don't display feelings comfortably will tend to have children who are afraid of their emotions. Conversely, fathers who talk about their feelings without inhibitions will set the example for their children to comfortably share their emotions.

Fathers need to make specific efforts to display love and affection to their children in order to leave a proper emotional legacy. Many of us fathers have made sure that our wills are properly written, but have neglected the most important item of all—whether our children are learning to receive love. We fathers should hug our children, touch them in appropriate ways, and tell them we love them on a regular basis. We may have to chase our teenagers around the house a few times before they will allow us to give them a hug, but it's worth every ounce of energy we use in the effort.

A father should not be afraid to discipline his children firmly, but he should also be able to listen to them when they are troubled. Children need outward and obvious indications that their father loves them unconditionally.

The following poem was written by a fifteen-year-old girl who developed a strong fantasy life, so strong that she also developed a second personality to help cope with the perceived lack of love in her family. She told me she could never recall her father hugging her or telling her he loved her. Yet he bought her all the toys and dresses she wanted. Her anger and confusion became so strong she would lock herself in her room, scream, bang her head and fists against the wall, and pull her hair. Here is her poem:

Breakdown

O God, for not another minute
Can I stand this crazy wreck of my life.
How I crave to be from this puzzling din cut—
Forever dead . . . forever free from strife.

Feel my tension building up from my toes;
Hear my weeping, tired and despondent dread;

Taste the salty tears of my depressing woes;
See the clumps of hair I pull from my head.

Whether lying here in a wretched heap,
or smashing everything within a rod,
I am all alone . . . all alone . . . O God,
Someone help me . . . lull me to eternal sleep.

Fathers, leave positive emotional as well as spiritual, legacies to your children. Don't leave these treasured responsibilities to someone else by default. You can have a significant influence in teaching your children how to give and receive love. It begins by making sure of your ability to give love in ways they can appreciate.

OTHER COMPONENTS OF THE SENSE OF BEING

Learning to love ourselves and learning to accept God's love is the foundation of a complete sense of being. But once this is established, there are additional building blocks to add in response to the question, "Who am I?"

● *Interests.* Interests are the likes and dislikes each of us develop over our lifetimes. One person prefers math and science courses in school, while another student likes art and drama. Some people enjoy working with their hands; others like to talk about abstract ideas.

While interests do not necessarily include actual abilities or aptitudes, it is common for us to prefer those activities in which we are most successful. An accurate picture of our interest patterns is helpful in directing us to areas in which we are more likely to find educational, vocational, or personal satisfaction.

I graduated from a small Christian high school thinking I wanted to be an electrical engineer. I had never talked to a guidance counselor about the appropriateness of my goals because our school didn't have one. During my first two quarters at Oregon State University, engineering lost its appeal. My previous certainty about my college major became clouded. Electrical engineering was not my calling, but I had no idea of what to put in its place.

I went to the university counseling center and presented my dilemma. After completing some interest and personality tests and discussing them with the counselor, a clearer picture of my real interests emerged. I preferred working with people rather than circuit diagrams. Though I enjoy working with my hands in my hobbies, electrical engineering wasn't an appropriate vocational goal. I enjoy outdoor activities for recreation, but prefer to carry out most of my professional activities inside. The abstract concepts inherent in psychology were more interesting than a math equation.

I eventually decided to pursue psychology rather than engineering. Psychology was much more consistent with my interests and abilities. My parents breathed a sigh of relief. During high school, they had watched me repeatedly attempt to fix the taillights on my car or to hook up the directional signals on our boat trailer. Consistently, I managed to blow out every fuse or mix up every wire in sight! Truly, electricity and I didn't make proper connections. It would have been a very unenlightening union.

● *Abilities.* A complete awareness of our sense of being also includes the recognition of our strengths—skills, talents, aptitudes, and abilities. Some abilities may be given at birth; others are acquired through experience. Whatever the source, we have God's promise that He will work through us regardless of circumstances (1 Cor. 15:58; Eph. 3:16; Heb. 13:20-21; 2 Peter 1:3-8).

A useful format for examining our strengths is to place five columns on a piece of paper with the following headings:

INTELLECTUAL SOCIAL EMOTIONAL PHYSICAL SPIRITUAL

Proceed by listing all of the positive skills, abilities, or traits under the respective headings. The following descriptions may be helpful in placing your strengths in the different categories. Many abilities overlap, so don't be afraid to arbitrarily place a given strength in whatever column seems most appropriate.

Intellectual—Knowledge that you possess; classes in which you have been successful; your style of learning or how you go about solving problems; information you have learned that is useful to you or those around you.

Social—Skills in relating to people; attributes that show up when interacting with others; leadership ability; practical skills that involve social contexts.

Emotional—Personality characteristics, traits, temperaments, and behavior qualities that are visible to other people; methods of coping with emotional problems; emotional tendencies that are of value to you.

Physical—Body features and appearance; skills that involve fine or gross motor coordination; abilities in crafts, mechanics, art, music, or athletics.

Spiritual—Qualities of character, discipline, motivation, intention, and maturity that relate to an understanding of God and His plan for you.

This exercise should give you a start in assessing your personal strengths. You could also give this assignment to someone who knows you quite well and see if he or she can identify strengths that you have overlooked.

If you are interested in additional tools for identifying and organizing your interests, talents, and abilities, I recommend *Christian Career Planning* by John Bradley.[3] This well-designed workbook can help you identify qualities about yourself that are related to vocational planning and the world of work. Even if you are not choosing a career path, the self-evaluation procedures can expand your understanding of your abilities.

● *Spiritual gifts*. A final aspect of a sense of being is spiritual gifts. God has given each of His children specific gifts (1 Cor. 12; Eph. 4), unearned and provided by the Holy Spirit for Christian service.

A complete sense of who we are demands we have a growing understanding of our spiritual giftedness. It is important to remember spiritual gifts are separate from talents and abilities.

Only believers have spiritual gifts. Talents and aptitudes arise out of our natural·inheritance or acquired learning. Giftedness depends on God's provision, not on heredity or experience (1 Peter 4:11).

Talents such as musical or artistic ability, public speaking, mechanical dexterity, or athletic skills can instruct, inspire, or entertain on a natural human level. Spiritual gifts are given to evangelize or build up the kingdom of God. It's possible for natural talents to support our gifts. One may have talent in public speaking as well as the gift of teaching or knowledge. Often, however, God uses a gift when there is no human talent to get in the way. Gifts are different facets of our being and may operate separately.

There has been resistance by some churches to present instruction on the use of giftedness for building up the saints. But Scripture seems clear that gifts are given to all believers (1 Cor. 12:7), so our total understanding of who we are and how we fit into God's plan and purpose must include exploration of our own giftedness. It's very important for each of us to study the matter and ask for God's guidance.

The proper use of our spiritual gifts will not only edify other Christians around us, but will also contribute greatly to our self-esteem. With a knowledge of who we are and the ability to love ourselves, we can learn lessons about what God would have us do with our sense of being.

SEVEN

"I have brought You glory on earth by completing the work You gave Me to do" (John 17:4).

LEARNING FROM WHERE WE ARE GOING

There was once a young sea horse who left his home to find fortune and happiness. Since he didn't know where to look for these elusive rewards, he asked several other sea creatures as he searched. The crab, eel, and sea bass didn't know the source of fame and fortune either, but they offered to follow the sea horse to find out if he succeeded in his venture.

Finally, the naive sea horse asked the white shark the way to contentment and satisfaction. The crafty shark said, "Well, of course. Just go right this way," and pointed to his huge open jaws. The sea horse and all his friends blindly followed the shark's advice and were devoured as they swam straight into his mouth.

The moral of this story is: If you don't know where you are going, you're likely to wind up someplace else and not even know the difference.

Fortunately, as Christians it's possible to know where we are going. There is a general road map to follow. God *does* have a plan for our lives. The basic structure of that plan is the next major element of our discussion.

STEP 2: SENSE OF PURPOSE

The next step in developing a complete self-image is to address the issue of our purpose for living. The question is, "Why am I here?"

As I discussed in chapter 6, the first step is to become aware of our

85

temperament, interests, strengths, and spiritual gifts. The second step is to ask what God intends for this unique person He has created. A sense of purpose gives direction to our lives. Direction is very important. If we don't know where we are going, we may very well get lost. Knowing why God has placed us here will give us a compass bearing, allowing us to cooperate with His intention.

Genesis 1:26 tells of our assignment by God to have lordship over creation—"Let Us make man in our image, in Our likeness, and let them rule over the fish of the sea and the birds of the air, over the livestock, over all the earth, and over all the creatures that move along the ground."

From the beginning, God has given man the task of subduing and ruling over the earth as His representatives (Gen. 9:2; Ps. 8:6). We are here to be of service to God. We are called to worship and honor our Creator (Deut. 26:10; Pss. 95:6; 96:9). We are asked to be wise and good stewards over creation, just as a loving and obedient son would respond to his father (Luke 19:13; Rom. 14:12; 1 Cor. 4:2; 1 Peter 4:10).

As children of God, our destiny is to enjoy fellowship with our Father while standing in awe of Him as our Creator (Gen. 28:15; Ex. 25:22; Ps. 34:18; Matt. 28:20; Acts 17:27).

Our calling is to be God's representatives on earth. As stewards of all that He created, we have the major purpose of bearing fruit. "You did not choose Me [Jesus Christ], but I chose you to go and bear fruit—fruit that will last. Then the Father will give you whatever you ask in My name" (John 15:16).

This Scripture and others (Matt. 3:8; Rom. 7:4; Phil. 1:10-11; Col. 1:10) encourage us to use our abilities and gifts in service for others. Then the fruits of love, joy, peace, patience, kindness, goodness, faithfulness, gentleness, and self-control will be planted, nourished, and multiplied (Gal. 5:22-23).

This sense of purpose becomes our long-range goal. The nagging questions, "Why do we exist?" "What gives meaning to life?" and "Where is this all heading?" are answered by God's directive to bear fruit. Suddenly we know why God has placed us here. There is a road map and a destination to end the traffic jams of our lives!

Many people have achieved some degree of material, financial, or social success in their lives. They live in nice homes, pay all their bills, own their own companies, and attend the right parties. But there's still a void. Something is missing. Earthly goals have been achieved, but the question of their reason for existence still remains.

It is amazing to me how often intelligent, well-organized men and women will carefully plan goals for the intellectual, social, emotional, and physical aspects of their lives, but will totally neglect the spiritual dimension. The portion of our existence that influences the very depths of our being is omitted in favor of physical fitness, promotions, and retirement benefits.

A fully developed self-esteem that can stand up against the rigors of competition, changing values, and aging must include a solid sense of purpose. As we focus on the maturation process, knowing our labors are to result in love, joy, peace, etc., we will be better able to keep on course and fulfill our destiny.

There is no road to success but through a clear, strong purpose. A man without purpose is indeed like a ship without a rudder. But an individual whose purpose leaves out worship, stewardship, and fellowship with God is like a ship which has a rudder, but no destination.

● *Conditions of fruit-bearing.* If our purpose requires us to bear spiritual fruit, it follows we should be concerned about how to produce the most fruit. Naturally, our self-esteem will be buoyed if we see God honor the fruit of our labors.

Scripture outlines five conditions necessary to bearing fruit and fulfilling our responsibility to God.

First, we are to have contact with the Living Water (Ps. 1:3). Just as a plant must have food and water, we must have contact with Christ, who is the Living Word and the Living Water. This means we must make an effort to expose ourselves to God's teaching. We can't expect to sit facing the sun and somehow receive all God has for us through osmosis. If we expect to bear fruit, our first condition is to develop a taproot that goes deep and continues to grow and to seek, even to hunger and thirst after righteousness (Matt. 5:6; 1 Peter 2:2).

The second condition for fruit-bearing is to be receptive to spiritual things (Matt. 13:23). This means we must be open to God speaking to us. God can speak through His Word, the teaching of the church, the counsel of fellow Christians, or through prayer and meditation. The primary consideration is that we must *want* to receive spiritual instruction from the Lord.

87

I have heard people say, "I don't know why, but I just don't seem to be growing as a Christian anymore."

Often growth didn't occur because the person didn't *want* it to occur. If we do not ask for God's truth, it's no wonder we do not receive (Matt. 7:7; John 16:24).

A third condition for bearing fruit is the necessity to put to death the old nature (John 12:24). We have to give up the old life. We must let go of the old, nonproductive, carnal ways of doing things.

I was raised on a farm, so I am familiar with growing sugar beets, potatoes, corn, and wheat. Any successful farmer has to keep abreast of new agricultural techniques. Yet some principles remain the same. My dad planted crops in the spring; cultivated, fertilized, and watered them through the summer; and harvested in the fall. The seasons never changed.

In order to increase productivity, my father was always looking for new fertilizers, chemicals, equipment, and rotation methods that would produce increased yields. As a young person, I was aware of other farmers in the community who had certain ways of farming that remained inviolate. They were reluctant to give up old tools or techniques. As a result, their production was low and they suffered economically.

In the same way, we have to learn from the lessons God teaches us and give up our unproductive patterns and habits. Just because we have been doing it for twenty years doesn't mean it shouldn't be changed.

Herein lies a significant point of tension for many Christians—one that can lead to much confusion and spiritual uncertainty.

On the one hand, there is legitimate need to accept ourselves. Scripture states Christ accepts us as we are. He loves us with our imperfections, infirmities, shortcomings, and sinful natures. We don't have to change anything to be assured of His love. This half of the paradox states that we should accept ourselves because God accepts us.

The other side of the paradox arises out of the requirement to die to self. Scripture states we are to lose our lives for Christ's sake (Luke 9:24); to be crucified with Christ (Gal. 2:20); and to be dead and have our lives hid with Christ (Col. 3:3).

The tension is created because Christians have a requirement to *not* be who they are. We are told to die to self and to love ourselves. How can we do both? No wonder pastors' studies and counseling offices are full! We are asked to love and hate ourselves at the same time. It seems impossible!

The answer to this tension is establishing balance. The desired balance is like that discussed earlier in the description of worm theology and pompous power.

We are to hate the sin or old nature that's within us. Our basic sinful nature has to die. The carnal side, with its inclination to selfishness, evil thoughts, jealousy, envy, and corruption has to be crucified with Christ (Rom. 6:6; Gal. 2:20).

On the other hand, we are to accept and love God's image and presence within us. Our real value consists of our likeness to God. When our thoughts, feelings, and actions are inspired by God and express the thoughts and will of God, they have value.

Our merit does not lie in our aptitudes or natural abilities. Our eternal virtue doesn't lie in our skills, beauty, or accomplishments. Our stature comes because we are sons and daughters of God Almighty! God wants us to love ourselves because His image within us is worthy of tender care and proper nourishment.

This balanced perspective of ourselves is akin to the balanced attitude we parents must have for our children. We can be very displeased with their behavior, but still love them.

My sons, Bryce and Lance, may leave my best hammer out in the Seattle liquid sunshine for several days. When I see that hammer lying in the grass, covered with dirt and rust, you can count on me getting very unhappy about their irresponsibility and forgetfulness. You can also be sure that Bryce and Lance will hear about my feelings. They may also experience some natural or logical consequences as a result of the incident! But I will still love them.

If we can experience this kind of balanced acceptance for our family members, we can learn to apply it to ourselves.

Pruning is another of God's conditions for fruit-bearing (John 15:2). In John 15, God is described as a vinedresser, One who thins out the unproductive or useless branches on a grapevine. The word *purge* in John 15:2 means to cleanse from filth or impurity. This cleansing process allows more nutrients to flow to the remaining parts of the vine to make it more productive.

A weakness in our lives becomes an opportunity for God's pruning. Pruning involves the elimination of weak or useless branches or vines. God isn't going to chop off the strong fruit or limbs. He wants us to be more productive, so whatever He prunes is going to be for our long-range benefit. His purpose is to teach us the wastefulness of our ways.

My first job as a psychologist was with a school district near Tacoma, Washington. Every two weeks, psychologists from a number of surrounding schools would meet together for in-service training. We would discuss cases about which we were concerned, as well as other professional issues.

At the time, I was the youngest member of the group and perhaps a bit too eager to prove myself. When a controversial topic arose, I was seldom reluctant to give my minority opinion. Though I *intended* to be tactful and productive in my comments to the group, I experienced some feedback to the contrary.

In the process of conducting a session on psychodrama, a visiting professor asked each member of the group to evaluate his or her level of positive contributions to the meetings over the previous nine months. We were to represent our self-assessment by taking a standing position on an imaginary line indicating values from 1 to 100. A low level of contribution would be indicated by standing near the 1, 10, or 20 values. If we thought our contributions to the group discussions had been quite positive and meaningful, we were to stand near the 70, 80, 90, or 100 levels.

I assessed my intentions and perceptions and placed myself at 82. Not bad for the new psychologist on the block!

Then the feedback part of the process began. The leader asked the total group to evaluate where each person had placed himself. If the group thought a change in position was necessary, they were to assign a new ranking to that individual.

Guess what happened to the overconfident young psychologist? Because of my devil's advocate role and sometimes intolerant attitude, I was demoted to the mid-40s on the contribution scale. What a comedown! My intent and desire to be a cooperative and positive member of that group of psychologists was not coming across the way I had intended.

At that moment, some pruning began to take place. I became

aware of unproductive fruit growing on my vine. Those actions needed changing. Sarcastic responses to differing points of view needed to be replaced by the fruits of patience, kindness, and gentleness. God used my colleagues and that situation to start the pruning process.

Other people, including my wife, children, clients, friends, and the Holy Spirit, have also been used to teach me about useless branches. Whatever the tool, I am learning to be ready to accept the pruning because strength comes out of the process.

The fifth and final condition for fruit-bearing is to *abide* in Christ (John 15:5). The word *abiding* is used frequently in John 15. The word means we are to be always looking for nurture, contentment, and instruction in the person of Jesus Christ. We are to maintain unbroken fellowship with Him who is our source of life. We are to obey the commandments God has given us.

If we expect to bear fruit and find self-esteem in qualities of a permanent nature, we must abide in Christ. Apart from Jesus we can do nothing (John 15:5). We must maintain a continuous flow of obedient communication with our Lord. We are told to pray without ceasing (1 Thes. 5:17) as a way to ensure that uninterrupted bond of fellowship.

Notice the progression as outlined by the Apostle John. For our prayers to be answered, we are to abide in Christ and let His words abide in us (John 15:7). The way we can know we are abiding in God's love is by keeping His commandments (John 15:10; 1 John 3:24). One of the major signs of obedience is loving one another (John 15:17). Abiding in this way allows us to be called friends of Christ (John 15:14). As His friends, we shall be told everything that Jesus has heard from His Father (John 15:15). With that kind of close, intimate communication we can't help but bear fruit.

A plant will not grow if it is pulled from the ground. If a vine is removed from its source of food and water, it will surely die. Some Christians seem to neglect this necessity. They go to church once in a while and say that they believe in God, but seek no other fellowship with Him.

Friendship is difficult to maintain if we never communicate with that friend. We must have frequent contact, no matter how close the friendship once was. The same is true of abiding in Christ. We need to talk with Him in prayer, read God's Word, and fellowship with other believers as part of the requirement for bearing fruit.

These principles for bearing fruit can be extremely important in bringing about the abundant, meaningful life God has promised.

Our sense of purpose is fulfilled by producing fruit. Focusing on the nature of our fruit and principles for increasing our productivity will give us direction and meaning. We can know where we are going and how to get there. A major contribution to self-esteem and self-confidence comes as a result of this process.

STEP 3: SENSE OF MINISTRY

A sense of ministry asks the question, "How am I to serve?" and provides focus on *how* one participates in the daily workings of God's kingdom. Our ministry gives us a blueprint for carrying out our purpose. It includes our vocation as well as our function within the community of believers. While our sense of purpose tells us that we are to bear fruit, our sense of ministry gives us clarity as to *where* and *how* that fruit is to influence the rest of the Christian community.

This step in self-esteem is necessary because we are all called to be ministers and servants of God (Isa. 61:6; 2 Cor. 6:4). Each Christian is part of the priesthood of believers (Ex. 19:6; 1 Peter 2:5). This means there are no positions of "higher calling." We are *all* called to glorify God and to serve. As believers, we are all equally accountable for how well our responsibilities are carried out. A paid clergyman who serves full time is no more accountable and has no higher calling within his sense of ministry than is a Christian bookkeeper, fireman, or truck driver.

This principle is illustrated in the Parable of the Talents (Matt. 25:14-30). Each servant was given the same responsibility—to invest the money given to him for maximum yield and benefit. The master didn't expect the servant who was given $1,000 to make the same amount of money as the one who was given $5,000. Rather, he expected each servant to invest wisely and bring back the highest return possible in relation to the amount given him.

Each of us has been given different talents and abilities. We are exposed to different opportunities. The common task is to put to wise use what we've been given. The application of our abilities and gifts to the purpose of reproducing fruit is the fulfillment of our sense of ministry.

We are all full-time Christians; therefore, we all have full-time ministries. Some, such as pastors and missionaries, have been given special gifts to carry out their ministry. Laymen in the church have chosen to help support these "full-time" workers financially so their time is freed to give maximum effort to the task of evangelism, preaching, and teaching. But the layman is no less "full time" than the clergy in terms of responsibility to ministry.

Each Christian has been given gifts to complete the body of believers. That body could never be completed only by those publicly identified as pastors, Christian educators, evangelists, or missionaries. Every follower of Christ is called to some special type of ministry.

My own sense of ministry was made clearer a few years ago. A close friend of mine has been very successful in real estate and investments. For a time, I looked at some of the material rewards of his stewardship with a bit of envy. Then it became clear God had called my friend to a definite ministry and had given him the ability and gifts to carry out that ministry. Because he has been obedient to his ministry and has sought to bear fruit in his own way, my friend has been a good and faithful servant. But he has been called to a different ministry than I.

Let's say that God called my friend to be an apple tree. He is then responsible to produce the very best apples he can. For contrast, let's say God has called me to be a potato vine. Since potatoes grow underground, they aren't as visible as apples. An apple grower can inspect his apples any time by just going out and looking at the trees. But potatoes require that the grower go out and dig into the ground to monitor the growth.

Nevertheless, I'm responsible to fulfill my ministry in life by yielding the fruit of potatoes, not apples. The kingdom of God needs both apples and potatoes. One is not any better than the other; they are just different kinds of food. Some people will like apples, others potatoes. Both are necessary. In the same way, you may be called to be a dietician, computer programmer, homemaker, gardener, or fisherman. Each is necessary.

When I realized my focus of accountability was not dealing in real estate or high finance but working with people who struggled with emotional and spiritual problems, I was released from the tension of inappropriate comparisons. I am to minister to the emotional needs of people who seek my help, and my friend is responsible to help those

93

who have certain financial needs. Each of us is a full-time minister, but called to serve in distinctly different ways.

● *Importance of ministry.* It's often reported that the majority of workers in the United States are unsatisfied with their jobs. They put in forty hours every week, but live mostly for the next weekend and two weeks of vacation each year. Jobs are seen merely as a means to an end, that which provides the money to buy the latest technological toy, the vacation in Hawaii, or a night out on the town.

What a dismal prospect! Forty hours of drudgery to earn sixteen daylight hours of playtime. No wonder most workers are discouraged.

The risks of this type of priority system come to light in times of economic depression. If a worker loses his job, his self-worth is devastated. This is a very precarious position. And yet millions of people place their worth and value only on their ability to bring home a paycheck. Men seem particularly vulnerable to this predicament.

Thankfully, in God's plan of ministry, we always have a purpose. Working for a paycheck or not, we still have a function.

There are several New Testament meanings to the term *ministry.* These include: (1) to promote the cause of Christ (1 Cor. 12:5; Eph. 4:12); (2) to cause men to accept the gift of reconciliation offered by God (2 Cor. 3:9; 5:18); (3) to cause men to be governed by the Holy Spirit (2 Cor. 3:8); and (4) to give something to someone for the relief of a need (Acts 11:29; 2 Cor. 8:4).

There are as many ways to carry out the implications of these functions as there are people in the church. Space does not permit a detailed examination of how the different ministries can be implemented. My point is that each of us *does* have a place of ministry.

Regardless of our strengths or weaknesses, God desires to use us. The value of our ministries doesn't depend on our personal power. It depends on God. Knowing that God will use us in unique and particular ways greatly improves our feelings of self-esteem.

EIGHT

"I will give you the treasures of darkness" (Isa. 45:3).

TREASURES IN DARKNESS

"You seem worried," the counselor said to the anxious client.

"You'd better believe it!" replied the distraught individual. "I'm so upset! If anything else happens to me today, it'll be two weeks before I can get around to worrying about it!"

This could be the same person who said, "I feel bad when I feel good because I know later I'm going to feel bad again."

Worry, anxiety, and fear are some of the most common thorns. Who hasn't worried about financial problems, children, work conditions, or personal relationships? The possibilities for anxiety are limitless—freeways, failure, inferiority, teenagers, taxes, and time. Take your pick. They're all plausible.

Anxiety is the sludge of life. It slows our growth, tarnishes our potential, and weakens our power. Yet worry and anxiety are as much a part of our society as tranquilizers and TV dinners. In fact, the seventeenth century has been called the Age of Enlightenment; the eighteenth, the Age of Reason; the nineteenth, the Age of Progress; and the twentieth, the *Age of Anxiety*.[1]

An example of this age is provided by the young man who responded to an advertisement for an "Opportunity of a Lifetime." The applicant found himself in the presence of a very nervous employer.

"What I am looking for," said the interviewer, "is someone to do all of my worrying. Your job will be to shoulder all of my cares and concerns."

95

"That's quite a job. How much do I get?" asked the young man.

"You'll get $50,000 to make every worry of mine your own," replied the administrator.

"I'll take the job, but where is the $50,000 coming from?"

"Ah, that's your first worry!"

As common as worry is, you would think it's something of value. But worry is a lot like twiddling your thumbs—it gives you something to do, but it won't get you anywhere.

H. Norman Wright reports a study regarding the content of people's worries. The study found 40 percent of all worries were about things in the future that never happen. Thirty percent concerned things that were in the past and couldn't be changed. Needless concern about health occupied 12 percent of the worries; another 10 percent were categorized as petty, insignificant things that were not worth the effort.

Only 8 percent of all worry had a legitimate basis for concern.[2] This data suggests we waste too much time worrying about situations which we shouldn't worry about or over which we have no control.

It's the combination of these two attributes of worry and anxiety—common, but unproductive—that make this discussion necessary. For it is out of the darkness of excess worry that some valuable lessons can be learned.

LIGHT IN THE DARKNESS

"I will give you the treasures of darkness, riches stored in secret places, so that you may know that I am the Lord, the God of Israel, who calls you by name" (Isa. 45:3).

These words were given by God to Cyrus, a heathen ruler whom God used to help free the Children of Israel from captivity in Babylon. Even though Cyrus did not believe in God, he was used as a vessel for obtaining freedom. In a parallel way, we will see that God doesn't want us to be anxious or worried. But even when we are, He can show us that He is the Lord God of our lives.

Darkness can bring both healing and perspective not found in the light. Darkness can have meaning and purpose of its own. It is not just a neutral interlude until the next period of light. Darkness is a necessary component in the cycle of living.

This is illustrated in the natural cycle for plants. Darkness is necessary to produce the bloom in many flowers. The technical term for this is *photoperiodism*. Commercial growers of chrysanthemums are able to use this principle to produce flowers throughout the year. The key is controlling the amount of darkness, not light. Artificial light is used to keep the plants from blooming until they reach sufficient size or until they are needed for market. Then, the light is turned off or the plants are covered with a black cloth to increase the length of night necessary to bring them into full bloom.

There's an important lesson to be learned in finding that God is as sovereign in darkness as He is in the light. His power comes through by transforming our understanding of the darkness more than by changing darkness into light.

ANXIETY, WORRY, AND FEAR

● *Anxiety.* Anxiety is a feeling of uneasiness, apprehension, dread, concern, tension, or restlessness. It's the anticipation of misfortune, danger, or doom, not founded on rational facts. Usually, anxiety is undifferentiated. It's fear despite the absence of any particular danger.

The anxious person usually has physical symptoms such as shakiness, jitteriness, muscle aches, inability to relax, and an aptness to be easily startled. Internal symptoms include heart pounding, dry mouth, dizziness, upset stomach, and cold, clammy hands. The emotional state is one of apprehensive expectation, hyperattentiveness, difficulty in concentration, and feelings of irritability and impatience.[*]

Anxiety overestimates the likelihood of any real danger or threat. I remember as a small boy going fishing with my father and grandfather and being panic stricken as we drove along some of the narrow, winding roads leading to Idaho's high mountain lakes. To me, it looked as though the pickup was going off the side of the road and over the cliff at any moment. My mind overestimated the possibility of my father driving over the edge and plunging to the raging river torrents 500 feet below.

Sure, it could have happened. A tire could have blown, an axle could have broken, or a swerve made to avoid an oncoming logging truck. The likelihood of that happening was very remote. In my nine-year-old mind, however, it was inevitable!

A client of mine was panic stricken about the prospect of making a social faux pas. She was sure she would trip and fall in front of a group of people, or that her slip would show, or that she would make an embarrassing remark. Each of those things could happen. They occur all the time. In her mind, however, the consequences would be devastating. She was sure people would excommunicate her from the human race if any of these things befell her. She highly exaggerated the terribleness of the event.

As a result, she lived in constant anxiety. She continually dreaded that something bad was about to happen. Her generalized feelings of fear kept her trapped, even though the probability of something happening was slight. Even if some of these things did happen, the realistic consequences would have been insignificant. Even if she did walk into a room with an inch of her slip showing, most people wouldn't notice and those who did wouldn't care. Those who cared would probably tell her quietly—probably because they had experienced the same thing and lived through it.

Notice a familiar theme operating here—things are only as bad as we tell ourselves they will be. It's our misbelief or unrealistic appraisal of a situation that generates fear within us.

Scripture points out the appropriateness of realistic concern when it says we are to "have the same care one for another" (1 Cor. 12:25, KJV).

The Greek word *merimnao* is used twenty-five times in the New Testament and means to be anxious or to be troubled with cares. In the *King James Version*, it is translated "thought," "care," "cares," "careful," and "careth." In the later translations, it is translated as "anxious" or "worry."[5]

This type of continual fretting without good cause is denounced in such passages as "Why do you worry?" (Luke 12:26) and "Do not be anxious about anything" (Phil. 4:6).

● *Worry.* Worry is often used interchangeably with anxiety, but does have a different technical meaning. Worry is uncertainty about our ability to prevent something bad from occurring. It's a feeling of fretting or overconcern. Worry is usually tied to a specific event or circumstance. To worry about how to pay this month's bills or to stew about your teenager who's not home by midnight are common examples.

Worry is future oriented. It is an attempt to fret about the future just as guilt is an attempt to redo the past. Whereas legitimate concern should prompt us to take appropriate action, worry tends to create a divided mind which results in paralysis. Concern allows us to focus on behavior and events that can be controlled, while worry stews about circumstances beyond our control.[6] Worry is an overemphasis on "What if?" "What if I make a mistake?" "What if he doesn't like me?" "What if they have an accident?" "What if the sky falls in?"

These "What if?" questions are an attempt to imagine the future. We dwell on the worst possible outcomes, sometimes using our imagination to create the vivid details of the disaster. In our mind, we visualize the crash scene in all its gory details as we lie in bed fretting about our teenage son's late arrival.

● *Fear.* Fear is an emotion of agitation or fright caused by the perceived presence of danger or pain. The word used in the New Testament is *phobos* or *phobeo* and means to be alarmed, frightened, fearful, or filled with terror.[7]

Fear is usually stimulated by a real threat to one's physical or emotional well-being. If the neighbor's 200-pound Great Dane comes angrily after you on the way to the mailbox, baring his teeth and eyeing your ankle bone, you probably have a legitimate reason to be afraid!

The Prophet Habakkuk described his feelings at the prospect of the Chaldean invasion of Judah in the following manner: "I heard and my heart pounded, my lips quivered at the sound; decay crept into my bones, and my legs trembled" (Hab. 3:16a).

Fear is a legitimate survival response. It energizes us to flight or defense and helps protect us from harm. The physical responses are similar to those found in stress reactions. The body may sweat, the heart pounds hard, skin becomes pale and cool, hair stands on end, and the blood pressure rises. The muscles may get tense, along with dryness and tightness of the throat and mouth, an increased need to eliminate body waste, butterflies in the stomach, and difficulty in breathing.

A comment of clarification: Fear of the Lord is a different, but beneficial, type of fear. It can be defined as awe or profound reverence, and includes veneration, honor, respect, and acts of obedience. To fear God is a very healthy response. Job was "blameless and upright; he feared God and shunned evil" (Job 1:1). Solomon wrote, "The fear of the Lord adds length to life" (Prov. 10:27).

COMPONENTS OF WORRY AND ANXIETY

Recall Abraham, whose dubious trait of worry I briefly discussed in chapter 2. From his introduction in Genesis 11 to his death in Genesis 25 are ten recorded occasions when Abraham worried to excess. Only God knows how many day-to-day instances were left out of the Scripture record!

The major ingredient in Abraham's anxiety was the tendency to make absolutes out of possibilities. Even though it was unlikely, based on his history of success, Abraham believed danger was inevitable. For example, he was sure the loss of one water well would spell the destruction of all his herds (Gen. 21:25).

This is like worrying about whether we will have enough money or food next year even though we have never gone without before.

To make absolutes out of possibilities is sure to give anxiety a stronghold in our lives. "My child will surely fall and break his arm while playing on the swing set." "The ladies at the luncheon will not like the casserole I brought." "The boss (or teacher) will be dissatisfied with the report I'm giving tomorrow."

Dwell on these negative possibilities too long and we can contribute to their occurrence. What results is indeed a self-fulfilling prophecy. It's another application of, "You reap what you sow."

If we constantly worry about having an automobile accident, the probability of an accident increases with the amount of our worry. Job suffered a similar fate. "What I feared has come upon me; what I dreaded has happened to me" (Job 3:25).

If we give worry too much time and attention, like Abraham and Job, the odds are increased our worst fears will be realized. The best thing is to not trouble trouble unless it's truly troubling us.

Remember: Nobody has the power to make us miserable. We do it to ourselves. It happens by our unwittingly placing trust in an improbable future event. We are treating the "What if?" as if it were a reality. We're setting ourselves up to trust and believe in the worst possible fate. This is not what God intends. He wants our lives to be productive and enjoyable, not riddled with pain, discouragement, and failure. How much better to live by the self-fulfilling prophecy found in Proverbs 15:15—"All the days of the oppressed are wretched, *but the cheerful heart has a continual feast*" (italics mine).

● *Types of "What if?" statements.* There are four major classes of

73756

TREASURES IN DARKNESS

"What if?" statements. The first is *What if I get embarrassed?* We fear and desire to avoid any situation where other people may think negatively about us. This is a major source of fuel for maintaining anxiety. What will other people think? Often the modus operandi is, "Other people's opinion of me is so important I must do everything possible to prevent their ever thinking anything bad of me."

Isn't that a bit foolish? Who can please all the people all the time? Jesus Christ Himself couldn't do that and He was perfect! Yet many anxious people operate on the assumption that someday they will be able to keep from making any wrong moves.

A second type of "What if?" statement is, *What if I make somebody angry?* It appears Abraham didn't want to make Lot, Sarah, or Hagar angry. He wanted perfect peace at all costs. It's a guarantee of emotional paralysis to believe we should never irritate others. Life demands risks and sometimes our admonitions will help another person to grow, even if his initial response is anger.

I told a client some things about himself he didn't like. He stormed out of the counseling office and even called me afterward to tell me how uncaring and unsympathetic I had been. A few weeks later, however, he contacted me to acknowledge the truth of those observations. He expressed his appreciation for my willingness to speak the truth even at the risk of his anger.

If I had operated on the principle that I should avoid comments that might generate anger, I would have avoided the confrontation. Subsequently, that client would have been deprived of a growth opportunity because of *my* problem of not wanting people angry with me.

What if I lose their love? is the third "What if?" category. This assumes that we are powerful enough to make another person love us. Unconditional love, at least, is a choice. Seldom will an individual action on our part totally wipe out another person's love for us. This statement also assumes we must always be loved. Implicit is the belief we will wither away if we are not loved in the manner we expect. The only *real* emotional death comes if we fail to love ourselves.

The fourth type of "What if?" statement is, *What if I get hurt or die?* This anxiety motivated Abraham to lie about Sarah being his wife on two occasions. She must have been truly beautiful even at age sixty-five and ninety-five! But Abraham feared the two kings would

101

kill him if they knew he was married to her.

No one wants to die. Pain and injury are never desirable. To allow our minds to be constantly filled with anticipation of doom, however, will only give more power to the certainty of improbable events.

Now that we've identified the components of anxiety and worry, let's turn our attention to how we can cope with the presence of these thorns in our lives.

STEPS IN DEALING WITH ANXIETY AND WORRY

● *Step 1—Be aware of the feeling.* You can't improve your behavior if you don't know you're doing it. The first step in dealing with worry or anxiety, like any other problem, is to tune in to your feelings. Listen to your self-talk. Are you imagining future events and predicting the worst possible eventuality?

Remember: Part of the difference between worry and concern is worry dwells on the problem, while concern works toward solutions. If your attention is directed only to the possibility of misfortune, your worry meter is working overtime.

Listen to your body. Go through the following list of symptoms and underline all those that apply:

> Headaches; dizziness; feel faint; heart pounding or racing; shakiness; jitteriness; jumpiness; trembling; muscle aches; eyelid twitch; easily startled; sweating; cold, clammy hands; dry mouth; light-headedness; lump in the throat; hot or cold spells; stomach trouble; no appetite; bowel disturbances; fatigue; insomnia; nightmares; taking sedatives; drinking; feel tense; feel panicky; tremors; depressed; suicidal ideas; unable to relax; sexual problems; unable to enjoy self; avoid people; can't make friends; feel lonely; can't make decisions; difficulty in concentration; problems at work; inferiority feelings; home conditions bad; financial problems; impatience; irritability; feel "on edge."

This list is not meant to be a replacement for professional diagnosis, but it can be a starting place to determine whether your body and emotions are showing the wear and tear of excess worry and anxiety. Another idea is to start writing down what you think every time you feel worried or anxious. Keep it in the form of a diary or journal and write a paragraph or two detailing the nature of your thoughts. After a couple of weeks a pattern should emerge and you can tell whether your efforts have been directed toward solutions or toward problems.

● *Step 2—Determine the nature of your "What ifs?"* Ask yourself the following questions. Write down the answers to clarify what you are actually thinking.

—What are you worrying about?
—Is the focus of your worry under your control?
—What is the terrible consequence or result that you anticipate?
—What is the likelihood that your worst fear will occur? Even if the event were to happen, what would be the exact impact on you? Would it be as terrible as you think?
—Does your "What if?" concern:
   (1) embarrassment to you;
   (2) dealing with the anger of others;
   (3) the potential loss of love; or
   (4) the threat of pain, injury or death?

If you truthfully answer these questions, you should have a fairly good idea of how your worry or anxiety is structured and focused.

Anxiety by its very definition can be quite generalized. We can have a general sense of discomfort and tension without having a specific focus.

Thus, the two-step process outlined in the preceding paragraphs can be used to bring things into clearer focus.

First is our general awareness of the emotional and physical symptoms of worry or anxiety. Usually I get an upset stomach and tenseness in my chest, sometimes accompanied by a headache. At this point I know something is gnawing away at me, but I may not be certain what it is. Anxiety is present—a general state of tension and upset with no specific focus.

My conscious mind may not be aware of the source of the anxiety. But there is something going on that tripped the switch. Our feelings telling myself that created the anxiety. I just have to find out what it

103

arise because of how we think, so there must be a message I am is.

Next, we need to discover the thoughts that produced the symptoms of anxiousness. Usually I can review the past twenty-four hours and come up with the source. Most of the time, twenty-four hours is all I have to remember because I try to keep as current as possible.

The other day, for example, I found my stomach was a little queasy and I had lost my appetite for lunch. (Something really has to bug me to reduce my appetite!) I was writing a report at the time, so I paused to review the past few hours to see if anything had happened that might have influenced my feelings. After a few minutes, it came to me. During staff meeting that morning, another staff member said she had heard some negative feedback about some aspect of the counseling profession. She went on to describe the setting where she had heard the remark. Though the remark had nothing to do with me, I had hooked into it anyway.

At the time of the meeting, I thought nothing of the remark or how I had reacted to it. But at some level I had bought into the problem and was doing a bit of fretting at a kind of preconscious level. Once I stopped to analyze what I was thinking, I saw what had happened. Even though the situation didn't apply to me, I had started on a "What if they are angry with me?" thought pattern.

Immediately, I knew the source of my generalized anxiety. It now had a focus. Then I could eliminate the feeling because the facts didn't justify any more concern.

Worries are easier to deal with than anxieties. Once you pin down what it is that causes the uncomfortable feelings, you can begin the task of analyzing the validity and appropriateness of the worry.

At this point, we've dealt with the first two steps in coping with worry and anxiety. In the next chapter, we'll climb the final two steps toward replacing worry with something more profitable.

NINE

*"For Christ's sake, I
delight in weaknesses.
. . . For when I am
weak, then I am strong"*
(2 Cor. 12:10).

WORRY CAN
LEAD TO GLORY

The following poem by Grenville Kleiser provides insight into dealing
with worry by altering the way we think.

The Bridge You'll Never Cross
It's what you think that makes the world
    Seem sad or gay to you;
Your mind may color all things gray
    Or make them radiant hue.
Be glad today, be true and wise,
    Distinguish gold from dross;
Waste neither time nor thought about
    The bridge you'll never cross.

There's useful work for you to do,
    For hand and brain and heart;
There's urgent human service too,
    In which to take your part.
Make every opportunity
    A worthwhile gain, not loss;
The best is yours, so do not fear
    The bridge you'll never cross.
If life seems drab and difficult,
    Just face it with a will;

> You do not have to work alone
> Since God is with you still.
> Press on with courage toward the goal;
> With Truth your shield emboss;
> Be strong, look up and just ignore
> The bridge you'll never cross.[1]

The first two steps in dealing with worry and anxiety helped us identify the nature and content of our feelings of apprehension. Let's look now at how to change our thoughts so that worry does not maintain the upper hand.

THE NEXT STEPS

● *Step 3—Determine the truth or reality of your worry.* The most problematic problems are the ones that never come. Thus step 3 is necessary to eliminate the 92 percent of our worries which are insignificant, out of our control, water under the bridge, or events yet to come.

Most of us find the challenges of each day are sufficient. God hasn't yet made any superstar Christians who can fulfill today's duties on top of tomorrow's worries. Like Alice Hegan Rice wisely said, "It ain't no use putting up your umbrella till it rains."

One of the first things to do is to ascertain whether our feelings consist of legitimate concern or unproductive anxiety. None of us think we are illogical or irrational in our thoughts, so it doesn't do much good to propose the question, "Is my worry realistic or true?" We can shift, however, to a growth-oriented question such as, "Is worry helping me intellectually, socially, physically, emotionally, or spiritually?" (These are the same categories discussed in chapter 6.)

If our thoughts are helping, we should be able to point to some type of growth or progress in one or more of these five areas. If growth isn't evident, it's time to change!

Let's take an example. Lynn has decided to go on a diet. Over the past two months, she has lost quite a bit of weight but still hasn't met her goal of 125 pounds. The last couple of weeks, however, have not gone well. She has exceeded her calorie limit and even gained back a couple pounds. She feels anxious and worried because her family is going to Hawaii for vacation and she wants to reach her desired weight by then.

Lynn is aware of her feelings. She's also aware of her self-talk. It's goes something like this: "What if you don't lose all the weight you wanted to by the time you go to Hawaii? You promised yourself you would do it, so you would look nice in your new swimsuit."

But when she asks herself, "Is my worry helping?" the answer is no. The pressure she has placed on herself is impeding her progress. It produces anxiety which causes her to eat more. She then sees herself as failing, which leads to more worry and more eating. The vicious circle has started again.

Look at the consequences of your worry and anxiety. Make up a five-column sheet with the following headings:

INTELLECTUAL SOCIAL PHYSICAL EMOTIONAL SPIRITUAL

Write under each column what improvements (or growth) are occurring as a result of your worry. If growth is taking place, you have a chance to affirm yourself. If there is no growth, it's time to eliminate the worry.

A second question to ask ourselves might be, "Am I dwelling on issues from the past over which I still feel guilty?" Guilt, from God's perspective, is meant to be used as a brake or an accelerator. It stops us from doing things which God doesn't approve or gets us moving on things we previously haven't been doing. True guilt comes from a breakdown in man's dependence on God. It comes when we are convicted by God, alone, in our innermost hearts. On the other hand, false guilt is apprehension that arises when we have violated social suggestions.

True guilt is the kind described by the Apostle Paul, who wrote to the believers in Corinth:

Yet now I am happy, not because you were made sorry, but because your sorrow led you to repentance. For you became sorrowful as God intended and so were not harmed in any way by us. Godly sorrow brings repentance that leads to salvation and leaves no regret, but worldly sorrow brings death (2 Cor. 7:9-10).

107

True guilt results from divine judgment, not social expectations. Any guilt suggested by the judgment of family or society is false guilt if it does not receive inner support by the judgment of God.

If there is true guilt, the correct solution is confession and repentance (1 John 1:9). Then guilt can be erased and we can say, with Paul, "Therefore, there is now no condemnation for those who are in Christ Jesus" (Rom. 8:1).

Next we need to challenge the "What if?" statements. For example, would it really be the end of the world if your earrings didn't match at the ladies' luncheon or if your pants split a seam at the men's prayer breakfast? It would be embarrassing, yes. But you could live through it. It's not terminal to have mismatched clothes in public, no matter how chagrined you may be. A firing squad will not be called as a consequence of wearing one black and one brown shoe.

Worry is self-talk that makes absolutes out of possibilities. It is the choice of placing trust in the likelihood of some improbable future event. Trust should be placed in someone who has certainty and assurance. God is the only One who is absolutely and totally reliable. So the next major step in dealing with anxiety and worry is learning to replace unproductive worries with productive faith.

● *Step 4—Replace misbelief with facts and faith.* The key to eliminating worry is to place our trust in something solid, predictable, and helpful for growth. God is interested in our growth and He is faithful to help us with the process.

Earlier we looked at the occasions when Abraham worried. But now let's look at how his faith was developed. Faith doesn't happen by chance. It takes cultivation, partly by God, but with our knowledgeable participation. Notice the many times God affirmed Himself and His promises to Abraham before it finally seemed to take hold in Abraham's heart and mind.

After God first promised to shield and reward him, Abraham is said to have "believed the Lord" (Gen. 15:6). A short time later, God spoke to Abraham in a deep sleep, which started out as a nightmare ("a vision of terrible foreboding, darkness, and horror" [Gen. 15:12, TLB]—one of the symptoms of anxiety). In the dream God described to Abraham the 400-year sojourn the Israelites would endure before emerging four generations later "with great possessions" (Gen. 15:14).

Sometimes our own anxiety and worry can be like the darkness that came over Abraham. It may indeed be terrifying. But God promises to be with us and to care for us. How much better it is to place our trust in His promises rather than to make absolute probabilities out of vague possibilities.

Abraham was eighty-six years old when Ishmael was born to Hagar. Eleven years had already passed since God had promised him an heir. Another thirteen years went by and Abraham was then ninety-nine years old when God again repeated His pledge to greatly increase Abraham's numbers (Gen. 17:1-10).

You can't blame Abraham for being a little discouraged and impatient. It had been about twenty-four years since he had first been informed of God's plan. Usually we like things to move along a little faster than that! (Maybe that's where the county road crew gets its time line for fixing the pothole in the street near my house.)

Nonetheless, at age ninety-nine, the full covenant was given to Abraham, which included changing his name from Abram, instituting the rite of circumcision, and promising that Sarah would bear a son to be named Isaac.

Based on his close walk with the Lord, including the audacity to argue with Him about the destruction of Sodom and Gomorrah, Abraham has been called the friend of God (Isa. 41:8; James 2:23). You would think someone who had that close a relationship with God wouldn't trouble with worry and anxiety. Abraham continued to fret and stew, however.

God did fulfill His promise to give Abraham and Sarah a son, even though Sarah was 90 and Abraham was 100 when Isaac was born (Gen. 21:1-3). Here is still more evidence to Abraham about the trustworthiness and reliability of God. Surely this experience would do away with his doubt and worry.

Just a few verses later, however, Abraham was distressed again (Gen. 21:11). So God repeated His promise for the umpteenth time and assured Abraham everything would work out according to the divine plan.

Let's keep in mind that spiritual maturity is a building process. Let's not be too hard on Abraham. How would we like the whole world to have a written summary of *our* walk of faith? Compared to Abraham, our stories could be found in *Grimm's Fairy Tales*.

Now Abraham comes to the refining part of his growth process.

God decided to test Abraham (Gen. 22:1). The Lord told him to take Isaac to the land of Moriah (about fifty miles, a three-day journey) and there offer his son as a burnt offering.

Based on past experience, we might expect Abraham to really turn up the volume on his worry meter. But at this point, he was obedient. Abraham responded in action. He did what God told him to do. Abraham's faith was strong and optimistic. He even told his servants that he and Isaac would worship "and then *we* will come back to you" (Gen. 22:5, italics mine). The *we* reflects his confidence that Isaac would survive the experience.

When Isaac asked about the sacrificial lamb, Abraham's faith again shone. He responded, "God Himself will provide the lamb" (Gen. 22:8). And the ultimate test came as Isaac was bound to the altar and Abraham prepared to slay his son in whom lay the destiny of God's covenant.

At that moment, God intervened and said to Abraham, "Now I know that you fear God" (Gen. 22:12). He had passed the test. There was no hint of worry or doubt. He didn't try to bargain with God and negotiate a reduced sentence for Isaac. Abraham knew God would provide and he responded according to that belief.

Our own faith will have its ups and downs, trials and tribulations, thorns and thistles just as did Abraham's. But we have a choice whether we will learn from those experiences. The choice is to depend on our own understanding and resources for solving life's frustrations or to trust in the Lord God of Abraham and all generations. "Trust in the Lord with all your heart and lean not on your own understanding; in all your ways acknowledge Him, and He will make your paths straight" (Prov. 3:5-6).

Our bodies will benefit as well as our souls. The aches and pains, upset stomach, nervousness, and irritation will all disappear if we place our trust in God instead of ourselves.

COMPONENTS OF FAITH

Faith is knowledge acted on. We must first exercise our minds and choose to believe God is who He says He is and can deliver what He promises.

Paul stated it this way: "For I know—I perceive, have knowledge of, and am acquainted with Him—whom I have believed (adhered to and trusted in and relied on), and I am [positively] persuaded that He is able to guard and keep that which has been entrusted to me and which I have committed [to Him], until that day" (2 Tim. 1:12, AMP).

Our knowledge is based on these facts:

- God cannot lie (Heb. 6:18).
- He has never failed to keep His promises (1 Kings 8:56).
- He has guaranteed to be faithful (Deut. 7:9; 1 Cor. 1:9).
- He knows our limits (Isa. 43:1-3; 1 Cor. 10:13; 2 Peter 2:9).
- He will deliver us from afflictions (Pss. 30:5; 41:3).
- He will comfort us in hard times (Isa. 43:2).
- His grace is sufficient for our weaknesses (2 Cor. 12:9).
- He will take care of our bodily needs (Ps. 37:3).
- He will answer our prayers (Mark 11:24).
- He will help remove obstacles (Luke 17:6).
- He will give us spiritual fullness and light (John 6:35; 12:46).
- He will provide power for service (John 14:12).
- He will give us eternal life (John 3:14-15).

Now that's quite a list of promises! The choice is ours. To trust in our own understanding or to place our faith in One who has never lied, never failed, and who has offered continuous help and security. That's a deal we can't refuse! Keep in mind, God doesn't promise to eliminate the problems in life, but to help us work through them to His glory.

An excellent passage of Scripture dealing with anxiety is Philippians 4:6-9. It begins by admonishing us, "Do not be anxious about anything." Next, we are told to tell God about our needs and to give thanks. And then comes the most important concept for this discussion. We are to let our *minds dwell* only on those things that are true, honorable, pure, and lovely. Here we have it again. We are to *think* of good things. If we think on the negative, our minds will be filled with worry and anxiety, depression and grief.

Listen to what God says in His Word about the importance of a sound and steadfast mind:

"A heart at peace gives life to the body" (Prov. 14:30).
"You will keep in perfect peace him whose mind is steadfast, because he trusts in You" (Isa. 26:3).
"Do not conform any longer to the pattern of this

world, but be transformed by the renewing of your mind. Then you will be able to test and approve what God's will is—His good, pleasing, and perfect will" (Rom. 12:2).

"Therefore, prepare your minds for action; be self-controlled; set your hope fully on the grace to be given you when Jesus Christ is revealed" (1 Peter 1:13).

The major step in replacing our misbelief is to claim the facts of God's promises, to place our faith in His trustworthiness instead of our own. Our prayer should be like that of the psalmist: "Create in me a pure heart, O God, and renew a steadfast spirit within me" (Ps. 51:10).

The next step is to act on our knowledge and renewed mind.

● *Step 5—Practice living "As if," not "What if."* Faith is of no value unless we act on it. The Philippians 4 passage ends with an emphasis on action. "Whatever you have learned or received or heard from me, or seen in me—put it into *practice*. And the God of peace will be with you" (Phil. 4:9, italics mine).

First, we are to think on those things that are good; then we are to act on what we know.

The same principle is seen in Abraham's life. Look at the action words in the biblical account of the sacrifice of Isaac. Abraham *rose* early and *went* to the place which God had told him. He told his servants, "We will *go, worship,* and *return* to you." Abraham then *took* the wood, fire, knife, and Isaac, and the two of them *walked* on together. When they got to the place of sacrifice, Abraham *built* the altar, *arranged* the wood, *bound* and *laid* Isaac on top of the wood. Then he *stretched* out his hand and *took* the knife to *slay* his son. God then intervened and provided a ram which Abraham *took* and *offered* in Isaac's place (Gen. 22:3-13).

Because of his faith in God, Abraham was able to take action. And because of the righteousness of God, any act of faith done in His name is valid, profitable, and useful for instruction.

Some concerned parents brought me their ten-year-old daughter who was suffering from extreme bedtime trauma. Somehow she had developed unreasonable anxieties about something dreadful happening if she were left alone in her bedroom. Her unconscious, but powerful self-talk message was, "What if something terrible happens to me while I'm alone in my room?"

The whole thing had gotten so far out of hand the parents could not leave her home alone in the evenings nor could Lisa sleep in her own room.

We proceeded according to the steps outlined in this chapter. First, we explored the nature of her feelings. To her, they were all very real: terror, horror, anxiety, and worry.

Through interviews and psychological testing, I explored what might be the source of Lisa's fear. Her family was quite stable and supportive. She was an excellent and popular student. She was a bit of a perfectionist and had a tendency to set high standards for herself and others. She was sometimes a worrier, but in general, was a pretty well-adjusted little girl. The only major problem was her outrageous fear of going to bed.

Next, we established the rational basis for her situation. By looking at Scripture and drawing on her own training, we outlined the promises God had given Lisa about His love and protection. I was aware that she and her parents had already tried this form of reassurance and biblical comfort, but I wanted to make sure the correct thoughts were being reviewed continually.

The final step was the most lengthy—changing her behavior. This had to be done in increments, so as not to overload her sense of safety and security. A tape recording was prepared which Lisa used to learn to relax her muscles and concentrate on God's protection. Week by week, Lisa literally moved her sleeping bag out of her parents' room, down the hallway, and finally, after several months, back into her own room.

Sometimes the progress was only a few inches. Lisa would decide if she was comfortable going to sleep at night in the hallway outside her room. "OK," she said, "but only if I can see my parents' bedroom through the open door." So she would take that sleeping position for a week or so, and then decide to move a few feet closer to sleeping in her own bed.

The process of desensitizing Lisa's fear took time, but it worked, and today she is a well-adjusted teenager. It probably won't be long before her parents will be worrying about their daughter being out too late and thinking of the good old days when she was afraid to leave their sight!

TREASURES IN DARKNESS: LEARNING TO GLORIFY GOD

The key to overcoming anxiety and worry is to place our faith in the providential and loving nature of God. Our natural tendency is to do things ourselves. When things go along rather well, we tend to get a little cocky and put too much faith in our own understanding. It is times like these that God allows problems to arise that can't be solved by our own stewing and fretting. It may sometimes mean eliminating access to human resources to allow us to be able to glorify God, even in our weaknesses.

The Apostle Paul had a lot to say about glorifying God in his weakness. But what does it mean *to glorify* something. *Webster's Dictionary* says it means "to bestow honor and distinction upon, to shed radiance on, or to transform into something more splendid."

This fits well with the premise of this whole book—we can be transformed into better people by experiences with thorns. God doesn't transform us by the elimination of our problems but by the renewing of our minds. Thus, most of the lessons to be learned so far have dealt with how our inner thoughts can be changed to produce a more productive mind. Now we will see how renewing our minds is related to glorifying God.

It sounds like a contradiction. On the one hand is the inability to cope adequately, but on the other hand is the suggestion that an experience of weakness can be transformed into something more splendid. How can this be?

The Apostle Paul said it best in a letter to the believers in Corinth:

> But He [the Lord] said to me, "My grace is sufficient for you, for My power is made perfect in weakness." Therefore I will boast all the more gladly about my weaknesses, so that Christ's power may rest on me. That is why, for Christ's sake, I delight in weaknesses, in insults, in hardships, in persecutions, in difficulties. For when I am weak, then I am strong (2 Cor. 12:9-10).

For Paul, weakness was an opportunity for Christ to show His strength. From this, we could conclude the weaker God's people are, the more conspicuous God's strength.

Malcolm Muggeridge spoke to this issue when he said, "Jesus is the prophet of the loser's not the victor's camp, proclaiming that the first will be last, that the weak are the strong and the fools the wise; that the poor and lowly, not the rich and proud, possess the kingdom of heaven."[2]

The reason God works the way He does is a result of human pride. We naturally strive for power and control. When we are in charge of things, we have a tendency not to need God. We get caught up in human understanding and take our eyes away from God, who is the source of all knowledge.

It's like the difference between a sailboat and a power boat. Using a boat with an engine, we can go almost anyplace we wish. Elements such as wind and tide are not major ingredients in how we plot our course (with the exception of watching for protruding rocks at low tide).

A sailboat, on the other hand, requires a more functional knowledge of wind and current. True, we have a rudder, but that only allows us to choose our course direction. The wind provides the power. The similarity to our daily lives is very close. The choice of how we deal with our thorns is ours, but the power is God's.

The Apostle Paul's experience teaches us periods of inadequacy allow us to be more conscious of God's strength and direction. He is saying, "I would rather glorify God in my infirmities than glorify myself in deliverance."

Paul wasn't some kind of nut who enjoyed pain and suffering because it felt so good when it stopped hurting. His rejoicing had a rational and sufficient basis. And it is just as sufficient for us. Because of our thorns, such as anxiety or worry, the power of Christ can come to rest on us.

The Greek word for "resting on" is *episkenose* and pictures God pitching His tent on the life of the believer. This suggests that Paul was asking to be made a dwelling place for the power of Christ. Our weaknesses then can become a condition for Christ's presence and an occasion for the manifestation of His power. All we have to do is choose to make Him a central part of our lives.

Many Christians think they have accomplished a lot just to admit to their weaknesses. A kind of resigned fatalism occurs where a person says, "It's just my lot in life to suffer for Christ. I don't know why God picks on me, but I guess I'll just have to go on suffering for the kingdom."

This kind of passive discouragement doesn't provide any basis for growth. It's like the person who says, "Every time that I think I get my act together, the curtain comes down."

More than resigned acceptance is possible. We can learn to rejoice in our afflictions because Christ is glorified. It isn't because Christ gets some kind of pleasure from our mistakes or infirmities. It is because when we are willing to acknowledge our limitations, we are ready to allow God's power to be manifested. When we have emptied ourselves, we can be filled by God.

George Matheson found he was going blind at age eighteen. Yet he overcame his handicap and became one of the finest scholars and preachers in nineteenth-century Scotland. He wrote:

> Thou, O Lord, canst transform my thorn into a flower.
> And I want my thorn transformed into a flower.
> Job got the sunshine after the rain,
> But has the rain been all waste?
> Job wants to know,
> And I want to know,
> If the shower had nothing to do with the shining.
> And Thou canst tell me—Thy Cross can tell me.
> Thou hast crowned Thy sorrow.
> Be this my crown, O Lord.
> I only triumph in Thee
> When I have learned the radiance
> Of the rain.[3]

God can and does heal. But there is occasion in each of our lives where we need to come to a point of yielding our right to be treated fairly and of demanding that God fix things immediately. We need to come to a point where we say, "God, I am weak. My anxiety and worry are overpowering. Come and dwell within me that I may rejoice in Your glory."

TEN

*"In your anger
do not sin"*
(Eph. 4:26a).

INSTRUCTION IN ANGER

Phil started to mow his overgrown lawn one day only to discover his mower was broken. Realizing his wife wouldn't let him procrastinate any longer, he decided to borrow a lawn mower from a neighbor. His initial thoughts were, "No problem. I'll use Fred's mower. He borrowed mine last year. I'm sure he'll be willing to lend me his for a couple of hours."

As Phil walked out of his yard, his self-talk began to take on a more negative tone. "Come to think of it, when Fred returned my mower, he complained it wasn't working very well. I'll bet he thinks I do a poor job of maintaining my equipment. Fred always takes such good care of his tools. He probably won't lend me anything."

Phil started toward his neighbor's house, but his pace became slower and more hesitant as his thoughts stirred up feelings of irritation and anger. "Who does Fred think he is, anyway? Maybe I'm not the best handyman on the block, but I do the best I can. He'll probably make some smart remark about the unsightly condition of my yard, along with everything else!"

Phil's stomach tied in knots and his anger level went to the red line as he rang the doorbell.

Fred greeted him with a friendly, "Hi, Phil. What can I do for you?"

To which Phil replied, "There's not a stinking thing you can do! I wouldn't borrow your lousy lawn mower if my life depended on it!"

Anger is a common emotion. No one escapes dealing with this feeling. Some people display their anger in more vivid ways than others, but everyone has experienced this unhappy thorn.

Anger has many forms and varying degrees. Basically, it's a strong, usually temporary, feeling of displeasure or irritation. Anger is an emotional reaction aroused when a person is interfered with, injured, or threatened.

The basic function of anger is survival. As such, it's important to realize the beginning stages of anger are automatic responses to perceived danger or threat. When a danger alert is transmitted to the brain from one of the five senses, a complex series of bodily reactions immediately takes place without conscious thought.

A physiologist, Kenneth E. Moyer, gives an excellent description of this automatic and involuntary response:

> Consider the caveman. The sight of an enemy or dangerous animal sets off a series of hormonal and physical reactions. Adrenaline pours into his blood, speeding up his heartbeat and raising his blood pressure. Available fuel entering the blood as sugar increases; the red cells flood his bloodstream to transport more oxygen to the muscles and brain. Breathing accelerates to supply additional oxygen and to eliminate carbon dioxide created by sudden activity. Blood ordinarily required for digestion is shunted to the brain and muscles. Digestion slows. Pupils dilate, improving vision. Blood clotting ability accelerates, preparing for the possibility of a wound. All this gears the caveman for action to protect himself. In this aroused state he can stay and fight if the odds look good or flee if they don't.
>
> Our bodies react the same way, though the danger is more likely to be a letter from the IRS than a saber-toothed tiger. And the threat doesn't have to be immediate to cause arousal. Merely anticipate anything unpleasant, perplexing, or uncertain, and you can feel the stress reaction go off inside.[1]

The lawn mower story illustrates that even the anticipation of an unpleasant event can trigger an angry response. Danger can be based on an actual or imagined threat. Whatever the case, it's real in the eyes of the beholder.

Anger is an immediate response to the senses alerting us to perceived danger. There's no time for deliberate thought initially. We are not so much responsible for *being* in a state of anger, as we are accountable for what is *done* with it. Once the conscious mind takes over—and that may be only a matter of a few seconds—we are answerable for how we deal with the anger.

Like depression, anger is not sinful. It's merely a danger signal. Once the alarm has been sounded, however, the difference between humans and a billy goat should become apparent. Anger is not wrong, but it can be harmful if treated carelessly.

BIBLICAL DESCRIPTIONS OF ANGER

Anger is referred to about 450 times in the Old Testament. The Hebrew word used most frequently is *aph*. It refers to the nostrils because the nose was thought to be the seat of anger. A person who was slow to anger was literally said to be "long of nose" (Ps. 103:8; Prov. 16:32).

Three quarters of the 450 Old Testament references allude to God's anger. God's anger is "kindled" in response to man's sin and ungodliness. Because He is holy and divine, God's anger must come forth as a natural expression of His just nature. A balance is presented of God's proper response to unrighteousness combined with His loving compassion and tender mercies (Neh. 9:17; Ps. 145:8). We should try to achieve this same balance.

Jesus gave further evidence that feelings of anger are not sinful. When he threw the money changers out of the temple and criticized the Pharisees for their stubborn hearts and hypocrisy, he was obviously angry (Matt. 23:1-39; Mark 3:5; 11:15;). Yet He did so without sin. The challenge for us today is how to overcome our primitive responses to anger and put away bitterness, wrath, anger, and evil speaking (Eph. 4:31).

● *Types of anger.* The New Testament describes four different variations of anger. The first is *rage* or *wrath*. The Greek word is *thumas* and it describes an intense, uncontained, explosive type of emotion. It's a lot like an eruption of the Mount St. Helens volcano in Washington—very little advanced warning! The consequences of this out-burst of negative emotion can be violent and devastating, such as murder or assault.

At a less deadly level, this anger results in the lamp being thrown across the room during an argument or the puff of verbal blue smoke that's unloaded when you hit your thumb with a hammer. In the Bible, a reaction of this type is found in Luke 4:28, when, after hearing Jesus denounce His hometown for rejecting Him, "all the people in the synagogue were furious" (see also Acts 19:28; James 1:20).

The next form of anger is *bitterness*. The Greek word is *parorgismos* which refers to a provoked or exasperated anger. This feeling comes from nursing a long-standing grudge. People with memories like ele-phants use this type of anger because they get a lot of mileage out of a very old irritation. Scripture clearly admonishes against such long-standing bitterness (Rom. 10:19; Eph. 4:26; 6:4).

Orge' is the most frequently used word for anger in the Greek New Testament. This is a form of *resentment* that often seeks revenge. It's like an overripe watermelon, which looks tasty but whose juice is bitter and harmful. Or like glowing coals or embers, which may look harmless but whose touch would bring certain pain. Like bitterness, this form of anger is also of an enduring nature, but a major differ-ence is the desire to retaliate or seek one's own form of justice (Eph. 4:31; Col. 3:8, 21). I should also note that two passages (Mark 3:5 and Eph. 4:26a) use the same word, *orge'*, but the notion of revenge is absent. This is a permissible type of anger since Christ is the One who displayed it in the Mark passage, where He confronted Pharisees who condemned the Lord's Sabbath healings.

The final form of anger is *indignation*, the Greek word *aganaktesis*. This type of anger results when an important ideal or value is threat-ened or violated. There is no desire to seek punishment or revenge, however, in this righteous indignation (Matt. 20:24; Mark 10:14, 41).

EVALUATING THE LEGITIMACY OF ANGER
The most important part of understanding anger is to determine if our feelings are legitimate. We get angry because an expectation is frus-trated. Breaking a shoestring as we rush to get dressed for church is irritating because we *want* to get there on time.

There are many things which can cause us to become angry. But when is our anger justified? Does it serve any useful purpose? God asked the same questions of Jonah, who was unhappy with God's decision to show compassion to the people of Nineveh (Jonah 4:4).

The following questions will help us reach a conclusion about the legitimacy of our anger!

● *What is my expectation?* First, isolate the thwarted expectation(s). What is the wish, desire, right, prerogative, claim, or need that has been frustrated? Write down this expectation so it can be examined in an objective fashion. For example, "I don't like it when a neighbor destroys my property. Furthermore, if my neighbor was unhappy about the fallout of leaves from the tree bordering his property, he should have talked to me about it first instead of chopping down the tree." Now we can proceed to evaluate the legitimacy of your feelings.

● *Was it real? Have I really been hurt?* Do the facts confirm our disappointment? "Has the tree really been cut down? Is, in fact, the tree on my property and not my neighbor's? Have I asked him why he did it? Could it be the tree was heavily infested with worms and needed to be destroyed immediately before the whole yard was affected?"

These questions illustrate how to go about checking out the reality of the external event and the relationship to our expectations. It's crucial to take the time to affirm things really did happen the way we first perceived. We have all experienced incorrect first impressions.

Your friend Alice did not speak to you as she left the grocery store yesterday and you're irritated because she snubbed you. Later, however, while talking to a mutual friend on the phone, you find out Alice had just received word her father had died the same afternoon her in-laws had unexpectedly arrived for a weekend visit. No wonder she was preoccupied with getting out of the store and quickly back home. Your interpretation quickly changes from thinking you were intentionally ignored to sympathy for Alice.

Sometimes the interpretation is correct. We may find things were indeed as frustrating as we had first thought. Analyzing our expectations doesn't take away all the hurts. But it's important to check out the accuracy of our interpretations before taking them any further.

● *Is the expectation useful?* Does the expectation contribute to our total growth? We can ask ourselves, "What specific goals for my

121

personal development are being blocked? Does it really matter if the expectation was not fulfilled?"

This may not be an easy question to answer. Usually we believe with all certainty that our expectations are wholesome and pure. The fact is, some of our wishes are selfish and destructive. Sometimes it takes professional help to unravel the productive from the unproductive. But clarity can be gained by asking ourselves how the particular expectation under scrutiny will contribute to our overall growth. Often our common sense will help us answer this question with sufficient objectivity.

If we listen to God's direction through the Holy Spirit, we can be assured of affirmation or conviction. All we have to do is ask for guidance, pay attention, and be obedient even if we don't like what He tells us.

• *Is it as bad as I think?* "Even though my expectation was not fulfilled the way I wanted, is there any way I may be better off because of what happened?" Our original expectation may have been perfectly sound, but the alternatives might turn out to be as good or better.

Let's say you had a goal of spending the weekend snow skiing with your family. It would be an opportunity to spend some quality time together participating in an activity you all enjoy. Skiing is good exercise so it would further your goal of getting in shape. Nothing wrong with the expectations so far.

Just as you prepare to leave, however, you hear on the radio that an avalanche has blocked the highway to the resort. The road will be closed for two days. You can't go skiing. Your whole family is angry! But wait, you have a choice. You can unpack the car, throw the suitcases on the floor, and be miserable all weekend. *Or* you can seek an alternate family activity.

Since you had told family and friends you would be gone all weekend, the phone shouldn't be ringing every twenty minutes. So how about camping out at home? I won't go into details, but I could imagine a fun weekend where the goal of family unity and fellowship could be achieved by some creative improvisation. If your disappointment over the initial frustration isn't allowed to keep you from considering alternatives, you might even be drawn together more as a family than if you had gone to the mountains.

Even when initial expectations are frustrated, good things can happen. You have to be ready to look for potential in the otherwise dark cloud.

> As you go through life, Brother,
> Wherever you may go;
> Keep your eye upon the doughnut,
> And not upon the hole.

Have you really been hurt as badly as you initially thought? Yes, it didn't go according to your plan, but in God's providence, is there a chance of a more beneficial outcome than you had thought possible?
• *Does it help me achieve fellowship?* We Christians are brought together because we share a common life in Christ Jesus. We are confronted with the job of learning how to love one another as members of the same family.

The Greek word for this concept is *koinonia*, our English word *fellowship*. God's impact on the world doesn't usually occur in isolated individuals, but within the fellowship of those who share that life in Him. "We proclaim to you what we have seen and heard, so that you also may have fellowship with us" (1 John 1:3).

This fellowship does require conformity to a standard—"If we claim to have fellowship with Him yet walk in the darkness, we lie and do not live by the truth. But if we walk in the light, as He is in the light, we have fellowship with one another, and the blood of Jesus, His Son, purifies us from all sin" (1 John 1:6-7).

We must walk in the light. We cannot lie to ourselves or to one another. *Koinonia* means association, community, joint participation, intimacy, and a unity of purpose. If we find ourselves experiencing anger because our expectations are not being met, it's important to ask whether fellowship would have been improved if things had gone according to our wishes.

When we begin to consider the long-term effects on the rest of the fellowship of believers, a lot of self-centered expectations should drop overboard rather quickly.

A group of college classmates decided to go on a rather long, difficult hike to celebrate the course's completion. The goal of the hike was to reach the top of a small mountain, but one girl who was

123

very much out of shape did not make it. The group had a common goal, but since there was a difference in ability, one person didn't reach it.

Fortunately, the story had a happy ending. The class realized unity was not served by the initial experience, so they decided to try again. This time it took four hours and many rest stops to complete the usual 1½ hour hike. But they all made it together. Some of the class may have been irritated by having to go more slowly. Their physical endurance was certainly not being tested. But because of the commitment to mutual success, some of the individual expectations had to take a backseat to the broader goal of fellowship.

When we are evaluating our choice to be angry, we need to ask whether our goals or expectations will contribute to the fellowship of the community of believers.

● *Is it worth the cost?* "If this expectation were fulfilled, would the cost to others be worth the gain to me? If I want my wife to keep an immaculate house, regardless of her energy level and time limitations, am I prepared to pay the price of her chronic fatigue and resentment?"

These are the types of questions that come out of an evaluation of the price that's paid to meet our expectations.

The trade-off between compliance and cost is often evident between parents and teenagers. Parents may demand adherence to certain values and standards by their children without providing the basic instruction or model for the integrity of those standards. If this happens, adolescents may comply, but the by-product may be rebellious or hostile children who don't do their homework or deliberately choose poor friends. Sometimes it's better to back off a preference for the short term in order to maintain a relationship for the long term. It's better to lose an insignificant battle, but still win the war.

● *Have I looked below the surface?* "I know what is bugging me at the moment, but is that the whole picture? I seem to be angry about one thing, but is that the heart of the problem?"

Very often something minor frustrates us and we dump the whole load because of an unresolved issue seething below the surface. This frequently happens in the instance of scapegoating. Dad gets "raked over the coals" at work, so he comes home and chews out Mom because the meat is overdone. Mom in turn hollers at the kids louder than usual because they are late getting to the table. And the kids, needing someone "safe" to pick on, go out and throw rocks at the neighbor's dog. It's an example of the pecking order in action.

Displacement is the psychological term for this phenomenon. One of the first documented instances of this defense mechanism is the account of Balaam and his donkey in Numbers 22. Basically, Balaam was angry at God for the way things were going so he began to beat his donkey (Num. 22:27). All of us have a tendency to look for someone besides ourselves to blame for our problems.

Back to the neighbor and the tree. I could indeed be angry because the tree was chopped down without my permission. At first, the anger toward the offending neighbor seems justified. Let's look a little deeper. As I think back, I'm aware of resentment that started when my neighbor returned the lawn mower two years ago with the comment, "I didn't want to keep your mower any longer, John, since I'm sure you want to use it on your own lawn!"

Maybe my own insecurity about my tendency to procrastinate is behind the irritated reaction to his comment. That was two years ago. Since then, he has complained about leaves falling in his yard every fall. Grudgingly, I must acknowledge I made no effort to trim the tree. Finally, out of desperation, my neighbor decided to take matters into his own hands. He chopped down the tree because I refused to take action.

What fuels my feelings now is the reminder, "Here again, I have disappointed someone by procrastinating."

Now we are getting down to the "real" source of the anger—passive procrastination. "I seem to eventually alienate everybody around me because they learn that I can't be trusted to carry out my responsibilities in a reasonable and timely fashion. It looks like the deeper issue is my own irresponsibility, not just the loss of a tree."

It may be risky to look below the surface. It isn't as much fun to look at our own inadequacies as it is to identify the shortcomings of others. The only way we can grow, however, is to be vulnerable and examine the integrity and in-depth accuracy of our expectations.

● *What does Scripture say?* Whatever else might be said about evaluating our expectations, the ultimate benchmark must be the Word of God. Anger is an emotion created and given by God. Yes, it can get us into trouble. But anger can also be a tool to energize us.

125

Remember: Anger is not necessarily a sin. We can disappoint God in certain circumstances by *not* getting angry as much as by over-reacting.

Charles Swindoll, in his book *Three Steps Forward, Two Steps Back,* gives some situations in Scripture where anger is justifiable. The following discussion draws on some of his comments.[2]

When we see a brother or sister in the Lord ignoring and knowingly disobeying the will of God, we need to be indignant. Moses had his successes and failures when it came to handling his anger, but when he saw the Children of Israel worshiping the golden calf, he got angry (Ex. 32:19-20).

Jesus was very direct with His anger while addressing the religious leaders in Matthew 23. Repeatedly Christ said, "Woe to you. . . ." and called the scribes and Pharisees "hypocrites," "fools," "blind men," "whitewashed tombs" and "serpents." That's pretty tough talk, but it was aimed at the sin and dishonesty in their lives.

God's anger is kindled by the ungodliness and unrighteousness of men (Rom. 1:18). We can be sure that God is angered when we choose to disobey Him. Solomon is a good example. He had been blessed with intelligence, riches, fame, and power. He had everything going for him. Seven-hundred wives and 300 concubines. His love life must have been nothing short of astronomical! But when Solomon got older, his heart turned away from God. Then we see God's reaction. "The Lord became angry with Solomon because his heart had turned away from the Lord. . . . Solomon did not keep the Lord's command" (1 Kings 11:9-10).

God is also angered when His standards are violated; for example, when the rights of the faithful and upright are denied (Isa. 5:23b). We should also be angry over injustice (1 Cor. 5:1-2; 2 Cor. 7:11), not with an anger that seeks revenge but with a motivation that seeks to correct the wrong. We are to be angry at sin but not to the point of hatred, malice, or resentment (Rom. 12:19; 1 Peter 2:23).

A positive example of obedient anger is Nehemiah. He was angered because some of the Jews had been extracting unreasonable interest rates from their debtors who had borrowed money to pay their property taxes to the Persians. Nehemiah's anger (Neh. 5:6-7) prompted him to call those noblemen together to urge them to implement a more equitable method for paying back the money.

A negative example is the anger of Jonah. He was unhappy because God chose to spare the lives of the people of Nineveh, Israel's enemies. Jonah preferred death to accepting the gracious will of God (Jonah 4:1-11). His was an anger of selfishness and stubbornness.

When we find ourselves overcome with anger, a major step in this process ought to be to ask if any of God's standards are being violated. We should ask ourselves where in His Word do we find the clear delineation of that standard. Then, through prayer, we can seek His guidance about our specific responsibility toward that situation.

THE PLACE OF FORGIVENESS IN ANGER

There are two ways to deal with pain and frustration, either by adding anger or by adding forgiveness.

Adding anger to a traumatic situation results in bitterness. I recall a client whose uncle defrauded her of $200,000. Though a Christian, my client was wasting untold amounts of energy in resentful thoughts about her uncle. Her own vast amounts of personal ability and creative potential were wasted because she was so consumed with bitterness.

If forgiveness is added to our initial pain, healing can result. What a difference! We can be transformed from victim to victor by the act of choosing to give up our right to judge the behavior of others despite the severity of the injustice.

Forgiveness does not deny the fact that another person was definitely wrong. Yet healing comes by actively choosing to give up the desire to seek revenge or to impose and carry out the sentence. Forgiveness involves canceling a debt (Matt. 18:21-35).

Forgiveness is an act of the will, not a result of feelings. Seldom will we *feel* like granting forgiveness to someone who has made us angry by wronging us. This doesn't mean we should cover over the feelings. It's very important to acknowledge our irritation, wrath, or indignation. But we are not to stay fixed on those feelings.

I have heard battered wives report their rage and intense desire to hurt their husbands who had inflicted bodily harm and humiliation on them. While I can appreciate the source of the anger, the wounds will not be healed by their becoming avengers.

The major ingredient in being able to grant forgiveness is to satisfy the basic requirement: *someone has to pay.* If my house is robbed, my child killed by a drunk driver, or my business embezzled, I want to be satisfied someone is going to pay for that pain and loss. A sin has been committed and I want a pound of flesh! I may know the money will never be returned, the child cannot be restored to life, or the memory never completely washed away. So I want to be assured some legitimate sacrifice is endured by the one who committed the offense.

It's against this backdrop of the desire for payment that Christ's death on the cross begins to take on new meaning. I've read many good things about forgiveness, but this particular perspective seems to receive little attention. A colleague of mine, Ray Struthers, brought this concept to my attention while he was working with several very traumatized clients. It was Ray's experience that many people have difficulty being able to forgive. Even though they know Scripture says they're to forgive others even as their Heavenly Father forgave them, an emotional blockage occurs.

Many of these clients had experienced severe and lengthy abuse earlier in their lives. And it was only when the substitutionary atonement of Jesus Christ was presented in a very down-to-earth manner that these clients were able to break free from the bondage of bitterness.

Isaiah 53:10-11 is a crucial passage in this discussion:

> *Yet it was the Lord's will to crush Him and cause Him to suffer*, and though the Lord makes His life a guilt offering, He will see His offspring and prolong His days, and the will of the Lord will prosper in His hand. After the *suffering of His soul, He will see the light of life, and be satisfied*; by His knowledge My righteous servant will justify many, and He will bear their iniquities (italics mine).

Because God is just, man's sin had to be punished. The spilled blood of animal sacrifices satisfied God temporarily, but we know from Hebrews 10:4 that "it is impossible for the blood of bulls and goats to take away sins." Finally, death, the ultimate price for an offense, was paid by the One least likely to deserve it—God's only Son, Jesus Christ. While it hurt the Father deeply to crush His perfect Son, it also satisfied Him greatly that the penalty for sin had been fully paid and justice had been served.

It's at this point that an emotional breakthrough can be made by those who harbor great bitterness because of injustices inflicted on them. Through the use of visualization, meditation on Scripture, and even symbolic action, the burden of anger and rage can be vented toward Christ's Cross.

Yes, somebody has to pay for the offenses imposed on you. And that "somebody" is Jesus Christ.

If you have had difficulty in removing your anger about past hurts, try unloading the burden of anger and revenge on the thorn-scarred head of Jesus. As impossible as it may seem, take God's perspective for a few moments. Place the source of your hatred on the cross with Christ. With all the imagination and feeling you can muster, vent your wrath in the direction of the cross placed on Golgotha almost 2,000 years ago. When your heart wants to strike out and physically injure your tormentor, imagine the pain suggested by this verse, "But He was pierced for our transgressions, He was crushed for our iniquities; the punishment that brought us peace was upon Him, and by His wounds we are healed" (Isa. 53:5).

You can actually find pleasure, as God did, in the substitutionary death of Christ. Not in some morbid sense of seeing someone die on the gallows, but in the sense of knowing justice has been served. Transgressions have occurred, but the price of pain and death has been paid. At this point you can be released from the stronghold of seeking revenge. Christ atoned for that person who offended you and you can emerge the victor!

ELEVEN

*Consider it pure joy,
my brothers, whenever
you face trials of
many kinds"
(James 1:2).*

PURPOSE
IN ANGER

Anger and conflict have been around since the beginning of time. Cain's anger led him to kill his brother, Abel. Abraham disagreed with Sarah over their sons, Ishmael and Isaac. Moses certainly had his problems with anger.

Conflict was present even in Jesus' earthly family. Remember when Jesus and His parents had gathered for the annual celebration in Jerusalem and Joseph and Mary couldn't find Him? After looking all over town, Mary finally found her son. Probably with more than a little irritation in her voice, Mary said to Jesus, "Son, why have You treated us like this? Your father and I have been anxiously searching for You" (Luke 2:48).

Christ's disciples found themselves in conflict over who would have the most status in heaven. Angry feelings undoubtedly arose during the discussion.

Some of these situations are examples of properly channeled anger; some are not. If we are created in the image of God, and if God and His Son, Jesus, experienced anger, there must be something beneficial to be learned from this commonly felt thorn.

The Book of James was written to first-century Christians who had experienced a great deal of conflict. They certainly must have felt angry and resentful about what had happened to them. The early Christians had been scattered by the effects of persecution. They faced discrimination daily. Businessmen lost their jobs. Their shops were

130

boycotted. Young people were kicked out of their homes because of their belief in Jesus. Children were teased and asked to leave their schools.

James was led to share with those believers just how all of this irritation fit into their growth as Christians. James 1:1 sets the tenor of what he had to say.

His greeting was, "Rejoice!" or "Be satisfied!" Rather an inappropriate way to empathize with a person who just came home from the shop which had been picketed all day and whose children had been told to stay away from school! Here comes a letter from this out-of-town specialist in matters of the faith, and he says, "Rejoice!" It's a wonder they kept on reading!

However, James continued, "Consider it pure joy, my brothers, whenever you face trials of many kinds, because you know that the testing of your faith develops perseverance. Perseverance must finish its work so that you may be mature and complete, not lacking anything" (James 1:2-4).

Two things are evident in James' opening exhortation. First, conflict and frustration are inevitable. James didn't say, "Consider it pure joy, my brothers, *if* you encounter trials." Rather, he said, "Consider it pure joy, *whenever* you encounter trials and conflict." The existence of frustration, which is the source of all anger, is not optional. We can always count on it being a part of daily living.

Second, James made it clear that conflict, suffering, and frustration are purposeful when he wrote, "The testing of your faith produces perseverance" (1:3). *Perseverance* means endurance, steadfastness, patience, or fortitude. It is the ability to be loyal to something or someone, even amid trials; to be unswerved from a deliberate purpose; to be persistent.

James' use of the word *perfect* (1:4) means "mature" and the word *complete* refers to "all" of our human and spiritual components. God's goal is to make each of His children complete, able to face any situation. God sees our inadequacies or areas of immaturity and often will move in to complete those qualities which need improvement. This growth may come about by learning to deal with conflict constructively.

At least seven learning opportunities can come out of situations in which we experience anger. If we are aware of the source and nature of our anger, these lessons can be additional stepping-stones in the perfecting process.

LEARNING OPPORTUNITIES

• *Opportunity to be energized.* Anger can have an important mobilizing function for us, moving us from apathy and indifference into action. Christians can sin as much from not getting angry when they should as they can by handling their anger inappropriately. We are told to "be angry" but to be obedient and not sin in the process (Eph. 4:26a).

Anger at dishonesty and sacrilege prompted Christ to chase the money changers out of the temple. William Booth, founder of the Salvation Army, worked day and night for fifty years in London's slums in the late 1800s because he was angry about the spiritual and economic conditions of the poor.

Currently there is a nationwide movement called Mothers Against Drunk Drivers (MADD) which is aimed at eliminating the thousands of lost lives, injuries, and property damage that result from fools who drive while intoxicated. The very title of this organization conveys the angry energy responsible for its foundation.

A local newspaper reported on an elderly man who hired someone to do cleanup work in his yard. One day later and about $1,500 poorer, there was no significant improvement in the yard. But thanks to the anger of his neighbors over the unreasonable charges and lack of results, legal action was initiated to get back the old man's money.

This kind of anger helps us to push aside apathy and fears in order to justify wrongs or initiate needed help.

• *Opportunity to release tension.* Repressed anger causes emotional destruction. Appropriate expression of anger clears the deck and provides opportunity to improve relationships. Expression of irritation releases energy that otherwise might go into harboring resentment. Repression of anger takes large amounts of energy just to keep a lid on things. If introspection shows our expectations are legitimate and expression is appropriate, energy is freed for more constructive, growth-producing activities.

William Blake, the brilliant but radical English poet and painter, captured this idea in a passage from *Songs of Experience*, written in 1794.

I was angry with my friend;
I told my wrath, my wrath did end.
I was angry with my foe;
I told it not, my wrath did grow.[1]

● *Opportunity to adjust.* Feelings and the physical symptoms of anger signal something is wrong. Our needs for survival, safety, socialization, or self-esteem are being thwarted or threatened in some way. It's an opportunity to locate and evaluate the source of the frustration.

Anger is like a toothache. The sensible person looks for the underlying problem behind the pain. There may be decay or lack of proper growth responsible for the irritation in the jaw. To ignore the pain just postpones the inevitable trip to the dentist.

The wise person who desires to grow looks at his frustration as a warning that there is a problem to discover, accountability and responsibility to assume, and steps taken toward resolution.

I graduated from a small Christian high school in Greenleaf, Idaho. I was what you could call a big fish in a small pond, and garnered a fair amount of success both academically and athletically. After high school I enrolled at Oregon State University, intending to major in electrical engineering and to play football and basketball. I had been offered academic and athletic scholarships at several smaller colleges, but I chose to go to OSU in Corvallis where my athletic accomplishments were unknown.

I learned a lot about unrealistic expectations that first year. I turned out for freshman football and found myself being the second smallest man on the squad. At 6'2" and 180 pounds I had held my own pretty well in high school. But my OSU teammates were 220 and 240 pounds! And they were mean! I stuck it out, even though I viewed most of the games from the bench for the first time in my life.

One of my most frustrating and discouraging moments was when my parents drove out to see their famous son play his first collegiate football game. I didn't get on the field once! All they saw were my warm-ups before the game. What a disappointment! As it turned out, my competition for quarterback later was awarded the Heisman Trophy as the best collegiate football player in the country. So I can't feel too bad about losing out to the best.

The next attitude adjustment came on the basketball court. Not having learned my lesson about unrealistic goals, I walked into the locker room for the first day of practice and ran into my competition for center. He was exactly one foot taller than I—7'2"! I knew then it was not going to be a very good day. Though I told the coach it might be best if I worked out at the small forward, not center, I still lacked the size to compete at that level of basketball.

Meanwhile, I almost flunked my first engineering math class. That left me 0-for-3 at the end of the second quarter of my freshman year. No football, no basketball, no engineering. My physical abilities, talents, and aptitudes were not matching up with my initial expectations.

I had several choices about how to handle the frustration. I could have blamed the system, wallowed in my misery, tried harder to overcome the barriers, or changed expectations. I chose to change my goals.

I had to make some adjustments. My initial expectations didn't match up with objective reality. Doubts certainly entered my mind. Several times I thought about tossing in the towel and going home where it was comfortable. But from this tough experience, I learned some lessons about humility, patience, and endurance. I also eventually saw how God could lead me by using both open and closed doors, *if* I was willing to take time to look for the lessons.

• *Opportunity to examine.* Feelings of irritation, rage, or indignation are occasions to examine the nature of our thinking. It's a chance to evaluate the exact nature of our perceptions and thoughts, to discover the roots of our anger. When we do, here's what we'll find:

First, other people don't make us angry. Feelings of anger are a result of *our* thoughts. Even when an event is unquestionably frustrating, it's our interpretation of that situation which determines our emotional response. We are responsible for our anger. It's another example of God giving us free will. If it weren't for our chance to choose, we would be helpless puppets whose strings could be pulled by other people's actions. We would be powerless to influence our own emotional destiny.

Second, examination will show some of our anger is a waste of time. Often, we have seen how anger immobilizes, contaminates, and leads to no productive purpose. If we look at anger as a chance to move on to creative solutions rather than dwell on the frustrations, we will be far better off. This readiness to learn from each situation reduces the sense of helplessness that occurs if we believe a situation is out of our influence. Resentment only makes us miserable, so why not get rid of it?

Third, the thoughts that produce anger often contain distortions, exaggerations, and falsehoods. Examination allows us to spot those distortions and to make adjustments that reduce the swelling. Often, for example, anger is intensified by a belief that the other person is being unfair. The more unfair we believe the situation to be, the more intense our anger. If we try to look at things from the other person's point of view, however, we might see how the judgment of unfairness was only in our own mind. Our judgment may or may not be founded on God's absolute standards. But as we examine why we think it's unfair, we need to be aware the other person does not share our evaluation. We need to be careful not to impute maliciousness into his motivation.

Fourth, we need to keep in mind other people cannot reduce our self-esteem. If we blame other people for our own feelings of inadequacy, we are deceiving ourselves. Other people don't decide our importance. Our self-worth is based solely on God's Word. "Don't you know that you yourselves are God's temple and that God's Spirit lives in you?" (1 Cor. 3:16)

It's not necessary to be liked by everyone. We don't have to earn the approval or acceptance of others. We are children of God and are valuable because He loves us unconditionally. Knowing this can keep us from responding in anger when people criticize or disagree with us. Defensive anger in response to negative appraisals by others is inappropriate, because only our own negative distorted self-talk can cause a loss of self-esteem.

Fifth is the lesson that can be learned from unmet expectations. When frustration is experienced, there's a 100 percent chance that we believe our unsatisfied expectations are appropriate and necessary to our happiness. Otherwise we wouldn't be angry because we wouldn't care. If someone comes along and removes all the dandelions in my yard, I won't be irritated at all. If, on the other hand, someone digs up the yard itself, I will be angry. Why? Because I expect my yard to look nice.

If an expectation hasn't been satisfactorily met, we can try to influence the external world to bring it more in line with our own needs. Sometimes that can't be done. In that case, we must consider changing our expectations. Anger can be an opportunity to establish new and more realistic expectations.

Finally, anger is legal. We *can* be angry if we want to. It's really quite childish to go around having a pity party for ourselves, telling everybody we have a *right* to be angry. Certainly we can be angry! The question is, "Will I benefit from my anger"?

Anger is a God-given emotion. To feel angry is not wrong. But we aren't necessarily supposed to go looking for it. There's enough Scripture condemning anger or telling us to be slow to anger to indicate anger is not a necessity. So, while we can be angry, we must also learn to keep it under control.

● *Opportunity to be assertive.* We have seen that anger can energize us into taking action we otherwise might not have taken. Once the adrenaline starts flowing and the blood keeps pumping, bold and assertive behavior can result. It can be very important to learn to take charge. How many times have we read or heard about a person being victimized and none of the bystanders taking action? We need to remember, "The wicked man flees though no one pursues, but the righteous are as bold as a lion" (Prov. 28:1).

I took a mountaineering first-aid class several years ago, and one of the major points was that in times of medical emergency, somebody needs to take charge. Someone may die if appropriate aid is not given immediately. This suggests two things regarding assertive action.

First, we must have the knowledge, so if we do take action, the help is appropriate. The final session of the first-aid class was to work with "live" victims at a Seattle area park. The class was divided into groups of four and we rotated through a series of different medical crises. On the third accident, my partners and I came across a victim with an open chest wound (faked). As we began to administer first aid, he began thrashing about wildly, making our task very difficult. Finally, the instructor came over and told us the way we were trying to turn the victim could kill him. Though the leader had taken charge, the nature of the assistance was almost more deadly than the injury.

Even if we are motivated into action, it doesn't do any good without the appropriate skill or knowledge to deal with the problem. This fact is not limited to first-aid situations, of course. I have heard

Christians jump to the defense of their faith, motivated by "righteous" indignation, only to find they had no substantial knowledge of Scripture to back up their statements. All they had were opinions and emotions. When we choose to be bold, we had better know what we're talking about.

Second is the obvious fact that somebody needs to take charge, not only in emergencies but for all of life. Many people are totally adrift in the sea of life. They assume very little responsibility, preferring to let someone else make the decisions and take the risks. Instances of anger can help us learn to take risks, to take charge.

Jimmy was deathly afraid to read aloud in his third-grade class. One day as his turn came to read, his eyes glanced to the floor as usual, his face flushed, and the teacher prepared to skip him again. But several of his classmates made some sarcastic statements about Jimmy's apparent inability to read. It had happened before and only served to make Jimmy more frightened. But for some reason, this time it angered him. He had always been a good reader at home or alone with the teacher. This time he vowed to show those kids he wasn't stupid. So he stood up at his desk, his knuckles white around the edge of his book, and began to read aloud. It was hesitant and jerky at first, but as he got into the flow of the story, his fluent reading skills began to show themselves. Jimmy went on to read the entire page with accuracy and feeling.

When he finished, the class applauded his effort and he smiled at his astonished adversaries as he sat down. From that moment on, Jimmy was not reluctant to read. He was initially motivated by anger, but the satisfaction of doing the job allowed him to continue. Anger allowed him to take charge where he had previously been unwilling.

● *Opportunity to learn self-control.* A friend of mine weighed himself on the scales one day, reacted with disgust and irritation about being twenty pounds overweight, and decided to go on a diet. Anger about his physical condition motivated him to change his eating habits for the better.

Often clients have come to me desiring to eliminate bad habits such as substance abuse, swearing, temper tantrums, overeating, or preoccupation with pornographic magazines. Almost always they would describe a recent event that precipitated an angry response and a decision to change.

137

A mother came to me thoroughly disgusted with the job she was doing as a parent and ready for positive alternatives. She was being highly critical and negative toward her young children—trying to control them with emotions rather than with firm and consistent consequences. Though her intentions were good, this caring parent had fallen into the pattern her own mother had used. Fortunately, her anger prompted her to make good and effective changes in her child-rearing method.

Even if we discover we've fallen into an unhealthy habit pattern, it can become a learning opportunity. All we have to do is choose to use the awareness of our shortcoming as a stepping-stone to maturity.

• *Opportunity to establish an interpersonal bond.* Unless we have experienced anger with a family member or friend, real trust cannot be established. Does that make sense? Think of it this way. Anger coming from a friend or spouse can be a gift. If the other person thought his anger would destroy you or the relationship, he would probably try to suppress it. But if you feel the heat, it's probably because your friend or spouse thinks you can handle it. Intimacy requires the full expression of all emotions, not just the pleasant ones.

The development of trust goes like this: If a husband gets angry because one of his expectations has not been met, he's likely to let his wife know about it, one way or the other. If things go well, they will be able to share their feelings and respective viewpoints and come to a mutually satisfying conclusion. Several things could happen. The husband could change his expectation; the wife could make a stronger effort to meet her husband's need—maybe she didn't even know what he wanted; or they could compromise. The process includes the expression of anger, but mutually satisfying results are obtained. Stored away in their respective minds is the message, "Hey, that wasn't so bad. We cleared that misunderstanding up rather well. I'm willing to do that again sometime."

A bond of trust is established and each successful expression and positive conclusion will strengthen that trust. A closeness is created because we learn the other person can be trusted with negative feelings as well as positive ones. The more complete the range of feelings and experiences shared between two people, the stronger the bond.

Just the opposite will occur if the situation is not resolved in a mutually satisfying way. The message in that case will be, "I'd better not say anything about my mother-in-law again because all it does is create hard feelings. Besides, my husband never listens to what I have to say. Negative feelings are something I have to avoid in this relationship."

Experiencing another person's anger tells us something about where he hurts. This is the flip side of our previous discussion about expectations. If another person seems angry toward us, it's because we've disappointed him. He evidently had expectations of us which we did not fulfill. If we can be objective and not hook into his anger, we can learn why he was disappointed.

This may open the door to our being able to minister to others. Our ministry could model Christ's when He met the raging demoniac named Legion, who lived in the underground cemetery. This man was so wild that he broke the chains used to subdue him. But Christ saw his need and cast out the multitude of demons that possessed him (Mark 5:1-20).

While we may not be required to exorcize demons, we can be ready to empathize with the hurts of others.

Part of my doctoral requirement at the University of Washington was to demonstrate a reading knowledge of at least one foreign language, in my case, French. I believed this was an archaic and unnecessary requirement, but I had to meet it anyway. Well, I took the French test the first time and didn't pass.

That didn't help my attitude one bit. I hated French! Why should I have to know how to read French anyway? Everything of importance in the field of psychology was already translated into English. I anticipated very few French-speaking clients after I graduated. Besides that, it was difficult!

I spent hours studying for the next test, but I failed it again. In fact, I flunked the test four times altogether! And the most discouraging thing was that my highest score came the first time I took the test. It was all downhill from there!

I never did pass that French test. The university initiated a policy change my last year of study which allowed a knowledge of computer language to be substituted for a foreign language. My petition for substitution of the computer language was on the dean's desk before the ink was dry on the new policy statement.

I don't know why I can talk to a computer more easily than I can read a French novel. But that's the way it is. And that's one of many examples I could give of dealing with frustration.

This type of experience provides a basis to relate to the many students I work with who have learning disabilities. It encourages them to know Dr. Martin had *his* problems in school also.

Empathy means taking on the feelings of another. It's what the Indians mean when they say, "Walk in another person's moccasins." Empathy doesn't require that I have all of the same experiences as my clients. This would be like saying a surgeon could only perform an appendectomy if he had taken out his own appendix. Empathy includes having experienced the same range of feelings, though the source and intensity of those feelings may differ.

Having experienced anger in many forms gives us an opportunity to share the feelings of others. Without this common experience, we would not be able to hurt where they hurt.

IT'S WORTH THE EFFORT

Each of us feels the sting of the thorn of anger. Some of those prick marks are small; others are large and unsightly. Regardless of our history and circumstances, anger contains lessons for growth. It's not easy changing old habits, but the freedom gained by being accountable for our feelings is worth all the effort it requires.

God's Word to the nation Israel, penned by Moses, summarizes what we've learned about anger:

> Do not hate your brother in your heart. Rebuke your neighbor frankly so you will not share in his guilt. Do not seek revenge or bear a grudge against one of your people, but love your neighbor as yourself. I am the Lord (Lev. 19:17-18).

TWELVE

*"And the truth will
set you free"*
(John 8:32).

LEARNING TO BE FREE ·

"I have come that they may have life, and have it to the full" (John 10:10).

If Jesus Christ came to give us life in all its fullness, how do thorns fit into the picture? Infirmities and frustrations in life are painful. Wouldn't life be a lot more enjoyable without them? After all, thorns are a result of the curse, not God's promises. Why shouldn't our goal be to remove as many of these weaknesses as possible?

These and similar questions may be going through your mind. Even after our discussion of the lessons that can be learned in the middle of our weaknesses, you may still not be convinced thorns are really beneficial.

To be sure, life would be easier without the limitations of fallibility. But we don't have much choice in the matter. We are stuck with thorns. So our choice is to take our lumps or learn from them.

Thorns can be very functional. On cactus, for example, thorns protect the succulent body of the plant from animal predators. And, unlike leaves, thorns don't give off precious water to the air. In the same way, we have seen how stress can teach us to be more dependent on God and how depression can help us learn to receive love and support from others.

This is not to say we have to remain content with the status quo and make no effort to improve our abilities or skills. Thorns are not something we necessarily seek. But since inability to cope in some fashion is inevitable, we might as well figure out how to make the best of the learning opportunities.

This brings us to the two major ideas we'll develop in our closing chapter. First, we don't have to solve all our problems before God can use us. Second, admitting our weaknesses and allowing God to renew our minds brings us truth and the freedom to mature.

GOD USES US AS WE ARE

A twenty-five-year-old journalist was struggling with his decision about a job change. He had originally come to see me while suffering from depression; now that problem was almost overcome, though he was not without his down times. He told me he didn't think he should decide to change jobs until he had *all* of his emotional and spiritual life together. I, on the other hand, encouraged him to confront the decision, not to delay it. He seemed amazed at the prospect of going ahead with his life while still having some problems.

It's true. God doesn't require perfect vessels to carry out His purposes. In fact, I don't know of any biblical characters who didn't have weaknesses of some kind. And yet they were all used of God. How can this be?

Look at David. His life was a strange mixture of good and evil. It was filled with noble deeds, fine aspirations, and splendid accomplishments; it was also stained with severe sin. Probably no biblical character displays such a wide range of moral and immoral behavior. The man who is mentioned as a man after God's own heart (1 Sam. 13:14) is the same one who committed adultery with Bathsheba and then arranged for her husband, Uriah the Hittite, to die in battle (2 Sam. 11—12). Yet Jesus Christ came to earth in human form as a direct descendant of David.

Samuel, the upright judge, was dedicated by his mother before his birth (1 Sam. 1:11) and then taken to be taught by the priest, Eli. Just how effective a teacher could Eli have been when Scripture says that "his sons brought a curse on themselves and he did not rebuke them"? (1 Sam. 3:13, NASB) Yet because God called Samuel, he matured and ministered for the Lord in spite of Eli's failings as a father.

Samuel served the Children of Israel well, but his own sons also turned against God, took bribes, and perverted justice (1 Sam. 8:3-5).

How could a man be so wise and upright, yet have children who seemed to be just the opposite?

Jacob, one of the two sons of Isaac, is a classic example of the conflict between the strong and the weak natures of man. He began his adult life by cheating his elder brother, Esau, out of his birthright through craftiness and deception (Gen. 25:29-34). Later, Jacob is honored as dedicated, prayerful, and faithful (Heb. 11:21). His life was a constant up-and-down cycle of spiritual success and human failure. Despite his thorns, Jacob was a chosen instrument of God.

Simon Peter was a man full of contradictions. He was presumptuous (Matt. 16:22; John 13:8; 18:10) as well as cowardly (Matt. 14:30; 26:69-72). He was self-sacrificing on some occasions (Mark 1:18), yet inclined to be self-seeking on others (Matt. 19:27). He demonstrated spiritual insight on some matters (John 6:68), but was slow to understand deeper truths at other times (Matt. 15:15-16).

Peter made two great confessions of his faith in Christ (Matt. 16:16; John 6:69), but also demonstrated a cowardly denial of that same Lord (Mark 14:67-71).

Peter's name meant rock or rocklike in Greek. Fortunately, when Christ said He would build His church "upon this rock," He was referring to the divine revelation and profession of faith in Himself, not the stability of Peter's human nature (Matt. 16:18).

God doesn't need a perfect man or woman to accomplish His purposes, only a willing and honest heart. The following poem by Sarah Ingham illustrates this truth:

Have you ever watched a potter
Fashion vessels out of clay?
He takes the formless substance
And in a wondrous way,
With patience, skill, and pressure,
Makes perfect works of art;
That which was clay is now a joy
To please the potter's heart.

So too the Master Potter
Takes clay so rough and rude
And fashions perfect patterns

143

From forms that have been crude.
He shows such skill and patience,
Uses gentle pressure too,
In molding lives for service
His daily work to do.

THE BONDAGE OF PRETENDING

The effectiveness of God's people throughout history has resulted from His grace and ability to use finite resources for infinite purposes. But there's still a human contribution to the overall success of God's plans. One of the major human elements is a lack of pretense. When David made an error, he eventually confessed it. He didn't pretend to be perfect. When the rooster crowed three times the morning Peter denied Christ, Peter remembered Jesus' predictions and wept bitterly (Matt. 26:75).

It takes a great deal of energy to pretend we have no human frailties or thorns. I think one of the reasons Peter, Paul, and Abraham were used by God was they were not wasting huge amounts of energy pretending to be somebody they were not. They weren't hiding behind masks of perfection, righteousness, or conceit. They acknowledged their weaknesses and moved on. Their honesty released emotional and spiritual power to better be used of God. These heroes of the Bible were not under bondage like the hypocritical religious leaders Christ so soundly criticized (Matt. 23:1-39).

Many times clients come to me with a problem they think has a physical explanation. They've gone to their physician for help with their upset stomach, headache, or lower back pain. Their doctor found no physical basis for the pain and told them to talk to a counselor. Often their opening line is, "I really don't know why I'm here. It's my stomach that hurts, not my head."

The initial interview often proceeds with their description that everything is just fine. Their children are well-behaved and good students. Their marriage is great and there are no problems with in-laws. The only problem is those constant aches and pains.

After much inquiry, there may come a partial admission, "Well, sometimes I wish my husband would talk to me a little more than he does. We have a fine marriage. We never fight. But we never talk much either."

Then the "real" truth comes out. Those stomachaches and head pain have to be caused by something. And the "something" is the bondage of pretending there are no problems when, in fact, there are a host of unresolved issues. But their faulty assumption is, "Christians aren't supposed to have problems," and the charade continues until their body can stand it no longer.

Denial presents itself in three disguises which I call: clowns, clones, and clerics. These impostors work as masks that keep truth hidden and emotional energy restricted.

● *Clowns.* Clown Christians are those who try to do it all themselves. They've gone to school and know all the right routines and moves. The world is their stage and they do their best to convince everybody that life is always wonderful. A sickeningly sweet smile is painted onto their face regardless of their mood. Their marriage or family can be a total disaster, but the performance for others continues. The show must go on despite internal pain. The mask must never be removed. They assume the truth would be too painful if revealed.

Notice how circus clowns are always on the move, never stopping, going from one pratfall to the next. This is also true for the self-sufficient Christian. He keeps on striving and straining, relying on his own energy and understanding. When the clowning Christian refuses to admit his weakness and dependency on God, he's likely to push himself so hard that a breakdown occurs.

Christians who strive to live up to the Christian standard on their own ability carry a heavy load. It turns out to be a yoke which they can't bear (Acts 15:10; Gal. 3:3), and one which leads to discouragement. The Christian life is a supernatural existence and can be lived only through the power of God (Phil. 4:13).

Victorious Christians are those who quit "clowning around," "who do not live according to the sinful nature but according to the Spirit" (Rom. 8:4). The solution is to choose to be dependent on God's power and not to lean on our own understanding. Our masks of self-sufficiency must be replaced by His loving embrace.

When we rely on the Holy Spirit for strength and direction, we no longer have to entertain or please the audience. In a real sense, we can enter into rest. We no longer look to ourselves for energy. Instead, we can trust God to supply the energy, ability, and guidance to deal with the thorns of life (Heb. 4:10).

• *Clones*. Clone Christians are copycats. They mimic what good Christians are supposed to do. Personal insight or individual study as to how God might lead in unique ways in their own lives is not sought. Instead, clones go to the recipe books and find out how other Christians live and then mindlessly copy that solution for achieving a life of devotion. There is no spiritual introspection, meditation, reflection, Bible study, or prayer. It is a matter of keeping up with the latest spiritual fad. What ever is "in" is the focus of the moment.

Richard Foster, in his book, *Celebration of Discipline*, both describes and provides a solution for the other-oriented clone:

> Many Christians remain in bondage to fears and anxieties simply because they do not avail themselves of the discipline of study. They may be faithful in church attendance and earnest in fulfilling their religious duties and still they are not changed. I am not here speaking only of those who are going through mere religious forms, but of those who are genuinely seeking to worship and obey Jesus Christ as Lord and Master. They may sing with gusto, pray in the Spirit, live as obediently as they know, even receive divine visions and revelations; and yet the tenor of their lives remains unchanged. Why? Because they have never taken up one of the central ways God uses to change us: study. Jesus made it unmistakably clear that it is the knowledge of the truth that will set us free. "You will know the truth and the truth will make you free" (John 8:32). Good feelings will not free us. Ecstatic experiences will not free us. Getting "high on Jesus" will not free us. Without a knowledge of the truth, we will not be free.[1]

• *Clerics*. Clerics spend the majority of their time telling everybody else how to do it. Definitely not limited to men and women of the cloth, cleric Christians like to *talk* about their faith, but don't do much *walking*. They teach classes on the devotional life but have limited experience of their own. They study the fruits of the Spirit, but are too busy to harvest any. They tend to spend more time promoting how to live and not enough time living it.

Christ was very tough on those clerics in Matthew 23 who put on a show with their loud prayers and religious pretenses. The scribes and Pharisees appeared to be righteous but were inwardly dead and empty (Matt. 23:27).

The all-talk, no-walk Christian is like the gluttonous man who passed out cards on the street corner saying, "Christ has answered every need in my life." Being at least 100 pounds overweight, he died from a stroke due to his high blood pressure. His claim was a lie. He was a compulsive eater and obviously had problems that were not being met. But his biggest problem was the refusal to admit he had any weakness. That denial cost him his life prematurely.

The German writer, Goethe, captured the essence of denial when he wrote, "None are more hopelessly enslaved than those who falsely believe they are free."[2]

The pretense that everything is fine regardless of the reality of pain or weakness keeps the clown, clone, and cleric in bondage to their denial. Like quicksand, their refusal to honestly deal with limitations drags these unsuspecting souls to the brink of emotional disaster. Eagerness to hide weaknesses often drives us further into them. Only when we bring those limitations out into the open and present them to God, can contentment and joy, rest and freedom result. Only the knowledge of the truth shall set us free.

TRUTH BRINGS FREEDOM

Freedom in the New Testament comes from the Greek word *eleuthros*, which means unrestrained; to go at pleasure, exempt from obligation or liability; or to be liberated.

Freedom is the ability to act or think without compulsion or arbitrary restriction. One aspect of our freedom is escape from the death penalty for sin because of the death and resurrection of Jesus Christ. Our confession and belief in the redemptive work of Christ gives us eternal freedom (John 8:36; Rom. 3:24; 5:15-18).

Another aspect of freedom is the unrestrained opportunity to mature. Spiritual maturity is the practice of using our powers of perception to distinguish between good and evil (Heb. 5:14). This completeness of growth is needed in order not to be tossed about by the deceitful teaching of men. We need maturity to discern counterfeit Christianity (Eph. 4:14) and to know God's will (Col. 1:9).

147

Maturity involves giving up old ways of thinking and developing ways of behaving that are appropriate for a Christian. It is the increasing ability to apply wisdom to everyday problems. The problems we have discussed in this book include stress, depression, poor self-esteem, anxiety, and anger. Truth, then, should allow us to completely and wisely deal with these thorns.

Christ calls people to what they can *become*, not because of what they have *been*. Our maturity comes from that same hope—in other words, not because we have done such a good job of solving all our problems but because of how we can learn to do it better. The hope of improved ability to cope is part of the gift of freedom.

This liberty gives us the chance to take risks we otherwise might not try. The principle many people operate by is, "Nothing ventured, nothing lost." If we don't take any chances, then we'll never risk losing anything.

A high school student reported to me her horror and embarrassment when, while in the sixth grade, she misunderstood a teacher's question and answered incorrectly. The class laughed and the already shy girl vowed never to volunteer an answer again. If she never risked making a comment in class, she reduced the chances of making a fool of herself.

That same vow of silence kept this bright young lady from developing her self-esteem more effectively. By never taking risks, she couldn't get feedback for good answers; in turn, the lack of feedback allowed her to continue to assume she wouldn't do well in class discussions.

The truth can come by renewing our minds and by learning the lessons from life's difficult times. It can help us break away from this kind of treadmill existence. God's grace and knowledge can help release us from the overwhelming burden of having to do everything right. We all have access to that freedom!

Imagine a couple of different coaching styles that might be used with a child who's having trouble hitting the baseball. The first coaching style includes a lot of criticism. The coach yells and makes fun of the batter's swing or stance. He shouts at the child to relax, to pay attention, and asks "Will you ever learn to do it right?"

Under those conditions, the child is bound to do all the wrong things. The coach's critical attitude is likely to produce just the oppo-

148

site result from what he wants because the batter will become so self-conscious and uptight that the instruction will fall on distraught and deaf ears.

I recall a nine-year-old pitcher in my boys' Little League experiences who broke into tears and wet his pants while still on the pitching mound because of the coach's hostile comments. The sadder part was that the coach was also the little boy's father.

But let's consider another coaching style. This one is based on encouragement, on affirming the batter's good qualities. The coach points out things the child could do better, but makes sure this is done in a context of praise, support, and good humor.

The latter style is more likely to produce a successful baseball player, particularly with young boys and girls, because the coach's positive attitude allows a child to be free to enjoy the game and to try new skills without the threat of undue criticism. The game is more fun, and in the long run, a better ballplayer results.

God uses the very same style of coaching. When we deal with the curve balls of life, we are to have confidence, not fear. If our background includes confidence to take risks, we will be willing to freely enjoy the challenge. We won't be panicked about having to do everything perfect. We'll be free to make mistakes which allow for growth.

It was Mahatma Gandhi who said, "Freedom is not worth having if it does not connote freedom to err."[3]

Similarly, John Keats, the English poet once said, "Failure is in a sense the highway to success, inasmuch as every discovery of what is false leads us to seek earnestly after what is true; and each fresh experience points out some form of errors which we shall afterward avoid."[4]

Experience is a valuable teacher if we choose to allow ourselves to profit from the learning opportunities sometimes called failures. Our eagerness to hide weaknesses often drives us further into them. But when we honestly acknowledge our thorns and deal with them face-to-face, inviting God's presence, we can become truly free. The bondage is gone and freedom is ours. Which shall we choose?

LESSONS THAT TRANSFORM

Let's review the lessons which can be gained from our experiences with weakness.

● *Stepping-stones to growth.* Thorns of inadequacy are painful. But the solution is not obtained by denying they exist. We begin overcoming our weaknesses by honestly examining ourselves. Then we can look to God to learn from the vantage point of our improved personal awareness.

Awareness begins by accepting the reality of specific inadequacies in our lives. Then we can explore the source of those weaknesses and make appropriate changes to become stronger, realizing God can work through us despite our emotional immaturity.

Nobody likes weakness. Society certainly encourages perfection. But when we learn improved ways of dealing with our thorns, the transformation to freedom can begin to take place.

An important ingredient in the process is to neither focus on the sin in our lives to the exclusion of good or to emphasize the positive goals to the exclusion of the reality of sin.

● *The growth principle.* Every individual, in order to function effectively, must feel that he or she is growing. Growth is essential. God wants us to grow up to the purpose for which we have been called. But it's risky. The alternative is to allow our comfort with familiarity to suffocate vitality right out of existence.

Stress can be either friend or foe, danger or opportunity. If we learn to make the appropriate adjustments to stressors, they can strengthen us, building muscle for the next difficult encounter.

The first step in dealing with stress is to be totally aware of our physical or emotional reaction to its presence. The second step is to make the best type of adjustment. Using the life of Elijah as a model, we discussed the following lessons:

1. God is no stranger to stress.
2. There are no limits to God's power.
3. We can't earn God's help.
4. God's help is immediately available.
5. We must depend on God, not ourselves.

A frequent thorn in our lives, *depression* can bring discouragement as well as teach us important lessons, especially learning how to receive acts of kindness and mercy from others. Depression can also enable us to empathize more deeply with others who hurt. The "dark night of the soul" can be an opportunity for us to learn to totally rely on God rather than religious protocol.

An important factor in developing positive *self-esteem* is realizing that God loves us regardless of our failures. Receiving God's love allows us to first love ourselves and then to love others. We must first know the facts of God's unconditional love, then learn to accept it.

The steps in building self-esteem include developing our sense of being, which asks the question, "Who am I?" Second, we must know our sense of purpose, which asks, "Why am I here?" Finally, we need to have a clear sense of ministry which asks, "How am I to serve?" Failure and frustration may cause us to ask these questions, but our self-esteem will improve by finding the answers.

The dark times of *worry and anxiety* can bring perspective that wouldn't be found if all were light. Again, we see God's power illustrated by transforming our understanding of the darkness more than by changing darkness into light.

The key to overcoming anxiety and worry is to place our faith in the providential and loving nature of God. It is out of the experience with the dark times that we receive the treasures of growing into better people. The transformation comes by the renewing of our minds, not by elimination of problems. In times of weakness such as worry or anxiety, we can learn to glorify God.

Anger can teach us much, but first we must recognize the nature and intensity of the anger we are feeling, whether rage, bitterness, resentment, or indignation. We must also realize that nobody else can make us angry—each of us creates our own anger, thanks to faulty interpretations, assumptions, and expectations.

A major step in dealing with anger is identifying the nature and appropriateness of our expectations. Then, based on the legitimacy of our anger, we can learn how to choose the most appropriate course of action.

Forgiveness is a crucial element in removing the traumatic sting from our memory. Getting past the roadblock that "somebody has to pay for the our hurt or injustice" is a difficult, but necessary aspect of forgiveness.

Several lessons we can learn from anger are:
1. Seeing an opportunity to be energized out of apathy.
2. Taking an opportunity to release tension constructively.

151

3. Learning appropriate ways to adjust to frustration.
4. Taking the opportunity to examine our perceptions and thoughts.
5. Learning appropriate ways to assert ourselves.
6. Taking an opportunity to learn self-control.
7. Learning to establish interpersonal bonds and trust.

We can indeed be transformed! The darkest times and the sharpest thorns contain learning opportunities. The value and impact of the lessons depend on our readiness to learn.

The following poem shared with me by a lady who was dying of cancer places a seal of gratitude on all that has been said:

I asked God for strength that I might achieve.
I was made weak that I might learn humbly to obey.

I asked God for health that I might do greater things.
I was given infirmity that I might do better things.

I asked for riches that I might be happy.
I was given poverty that I might be wise.

I asked for power that I might have the praise of men.
I was given weakness that I might feel the need of God.

I asked for all things that I might enjoy life.
I was given life that I might enjoy all things.

I got nothing that I asked for
but everything I had hoped for. . . .

Almost despite myself, my unspoken prayers were answered.

I am among all men most richly blessed.
                                —Unknown Confederate soldier

NOTES

CHAPTER TWO

1. *The New Bible Dictionary* (Grand Rapids: Wm. B. Eerdmans, 1962), p. 1273.
2. James Strong, *Strong's Exhaustive Concordance of the Bible* (Nashville: Abingdon, 1890).
3. Elizabeth Skoglund, *Coping* (Ventura, Calif.: Regal Books, 1971), p. 15.
4. Ibid., p. 17.
5. Ibid., p. 16.

CHAPTER THREE

1. C. Markham Berry, "Entering Canaan: Adolescence as a Stage of Spiritual Growth," *The Bulletin* 6 (4), 1980, pp. 10-13.

CHAPTER FOUR

1. Chinese calligraphy produced by Jonathan Pease, Department of Asian Languages and Literature, University of Washington, Seattle, Wash.
2. D.L. Dudley and E. Welke, *How to Survive Being Alive* (New York: Doubleday, 1977).
3. T.H. Holmes and R.H. Rahe, "The Social Readjustment Rating Scale," *Journal of Psychosomatic Research*, vol. 11, pp. 213-218.
4. James Strong, *Strong's Exhaustive Concordance of the Bible*, (Nashville: Abingdon, 1890).

CHAPTER FIVE

1. A.T. Beck, et al., *Cognitive Therapy of Depression* (New York: Guilford Press, 1979), p. 1.
2. Richard J. Foster, *Celebration of Discipline* (San Francisco: Harper & Row, 1978), p. 90.

3. Georgia Harkness, *The Dark Night of the Soul* (New York: Abingdon-Cokesbury Press, 1945), pp. 25-28.
4. Ibid., pp. 52-55.
5. Foster, *Celebration of Discipline*, p. 89.

CHAPTER SIX

1. R.L. Cramer, *The Psychology of Jesus and Mental Health* (Grand Rapids: Zondervan, 1959), p. 17.
2. James C. Dobson, *Straight Talk to Men and Their Wives* (Waco, Texas: Word, 1980), p. 69.
3. John D. Bradley, *Christian Career Planning* (Portland, Ore.: Multnomah, 1977).

CHAPTER EIGHT

1. James C. Coleman, *Abnormal Psychology and Modern Life*, 2nd ed. (Chicago: Scott, Foresman, & Co., 1956), p. 2.
2. H. Norman Wright, *The Healing of Fears* (Eugene, Ore.: Harvest House, 1982), pp. 59-60.
3. *Encyclopedia Britannica* (Chicago: William Benton Publishers, 1966), vol. 17, p. 1001.
4. *Diagnostic and Statistical Manual of Mental Disorders*, 3rd ed. (Washington, D.C.: American Psychiatric Association, 1980), p. 233.
5. James Strong, *Strong's Exhaustive Concordance of the Bible* (Nashville: Abingdon, 1890).
6. David Stoop, *Self-Talk: Key to Personal Growth* (Old Tappan, N.J.: Fleming H. Revell, 1982), p. 94.
7. James Strong, *Strong's Exhaustive Concordance*.

CHAPTER NINE

1. Walter B. Knight, *Knight's Master Book of New Illustrations* (Grand Rapids: Wm. B. Eerdmans, 1958), p. 757.
2. Malcolm Muggeridge, "Living through an Apocalypse," speech given at the Lausanne World Congress on Evangelism, July 22, 1974.
3. George Matheson, cited in *Till Armageddon: A Perspective on Suffering*, by Billy Graham (Minneapolis: World Wide, 1981), p. 90.

CHAPTER TEN

1. Kenneth E. Moyer, *The Physiology of Hostility* (Chicago: Markham, 1971), pp. 15-16.

154

2. Charles R. Swindoll, *Three Steps Forward, Two Steps Back* (Nashville: Thomas Nelson, 1980), p. 154.

CHAPTER ELEVEN

1. William Blake, "Songs of Experience," [1794], reprinted in *Bartlett's Familiar Quotations*, John Bartlett, ed. (Boston: Little, Brown, & Co., 1980), p. 405.

CHAPTER TWELVE

1. Richard J. Foster, *Celebration of Discipline* (San Francisco: Harper & Row, 1978), pp. 54-55.
2. Tryon Edwards, *The New Dictionary of Thoughts* (N.p.: Standard Book Co., 1957), p. 221.
3. Ibid., p. 220.
4. Ibid., p. 197.